The Citizen's Guide To Defeating the Mainstream Media

The Citizen's Guide To Defeating the Mainstream Media

Andre Harper

Published by
The Knowledge Movement Publishing

ISBN 978-1461044192

Printed in the United States of America

To Dana Loesch and Andrew Breitbart for all that you do to expose liberal media bias. Your relentless dedication and personal sacrifice was the inspiration behind this work. Although you take a lot of crap from the left, make no mistake about it, you are not alone. There are millions of us that stand with you.

"Andre's riveting experience boldly illustrates how the liberal indoctrination among black people and culture has done nothing but abandon them. Yet, he has been able to claim empowerment by breaking free of this indoctrination and embracing a more empowering one, one that will change the fate of his children's children."

Armstrong Williams, Nationally Syndicated TV, Radio Host

"I found Andre Harper to be honest and self critical about what it means to be a conservative Black Man. His views and opinions were outspoken and right on the money. He is an asset to America and to it's people with his honest look at American Liberal politics and Conservatives politics."

Bill English, Host, Plain English Radio Show

"Andre Harper is a refreshing new voice in American politics. His book, "Political Emancipation" is a must read for those who are disappointed in the current racial politics and are seeking a new perspective. Andre is a wonderful guest who will debate those who believe in the same old racist picture of modern politics in the African-American and liberal communities"

Speaking Of... with Mike Schikman, Host, 550 WSVA Harrisonburg, VA

"Andre Harper is a young man who has extraordinary insight into today's American political arena. His clear and precise analysts of complex political issues are invaluable. Through his intensity and unrelenting passion to help the masses, Andre Harper has dedicated his life to helping empower individuals and provide them with sound information backed by tried and true American principles of freedom."

Kariem A. Haqq, Founder of The 13th Amendment Freedom Week Movement

"Andre is a huge asset in bringing "Conservative Activism" to the forefront today. A leader in this battle to bring the values of truth, faith and courage to young people and teach them to live by conservative principles so they can live the American dream like himself. He rejected the liberal lies because he knows American is good."

Mary Kass, President of The Greater New Orleans Tea Party

"There are patriots and great patriots. Andre Harper is a great patriot. He represents conservatism, the Tea Party, and what American needs in a voice. In a day when the political environment is so energized with rhetoric and vitriol, it is great to hear a voice that breaks through all of the noise and sets the record straight."

Chris Pilie, founder of Lanterns of Liberty

"Andre's honest and bold perspective will continue to open eyes, and his impressive journey to conservative values will open the door for more young African Americans to be able to make the same connection. His work and activism is essential to the future of the conservative movement."

Wayne Bradley, Host, Conservative is Cool

"In the age of President Obama and creeping socialism, Andre is an unabashed conservative who has contributed greatly to the cause of ordinary Americans taking back their country. Having worked for a Republican United States Senator, Andre has an unique perspective on how a hostile and biased liberal media - can and does - shape the opinions of the masses. Great work Andre! I am proud to call you a patriot and a friend."

Christopher Arps, Co-founder, Move-On-Up.org

"Andre is a studly piece of delicious chocolate. Never one to back down from a fight, or conform to assumed norms. He's as inspiring as he is sharp."

Steven Crowder, Comedian

Andre Harper brilliantly dissects how those in the Progressive Movement have subtly infiltrated the black and poor society under the guise of social reform and equality. In his previous book 'Political Emancipation 'he started it and in his forthcoming book he ups the ante in the culture war. Andre's book is the next manual in addressing the progressive arguments. After reading this book you'll understand why Andre Harper has become an authoritative force in today's Black Conservative movement.

Stephanie Rubach, St. Louis District Coordinator
Concerned Women for America

Table of Contents

Introduction

After publishing my first book, Political Emancipation, at the end of 2009, 2010 presented me the opportunity to travel across the country and speak at several Tea Party rallies and other events. I met so many great Americans that care so much about the direction of our country. Many of these patriots, like myself, disagreed with the direction that President Obama and his legion of liberal legislators were taking the country in. When the liberal media and the Democratic leadership wrote off the Republican Party and thus conservatism, for at least a generation after sweeping wins in 2008, many conservatives understandably felt discouraged after such crushing defeats in 2006 and 2008. Jim Carville was so disillusioned by the election results that he wrote a book called *40 More Years: How the Democrats Will Rule the Next Generation*. His prediction was off by 39 years. You can now purchase brand new copies of his book on Amazon.com for as low as $.01 (which is still over-priced.)[1]

However, many of us refused to give up on our country or conservatism, and the Tea Party movement emerged across the country. This emergence resulted in big wins for the Republicans in the 2010 midterm elections. The morning after the election, Republicans gained 60 seats in the U.S. House of Representatives, with several more certain victories in uncalled contests pushing the total to the mid-60s. Although Republicans remained the minority in the Senate, they gained six seats across Illinois, Pennsylvania, North Dakota, Arkansas, Indiana and Wisconsin.[2] Not only did the GOP make gains in Washington D.C., liberalism was rejected from coast to coast. Republicans picked up 680 seats in state legislatures, according to the National Conference of State Legislatures -- the most in the modern era. To put that number in perspective: in the 1994 GOP wave, Republicans picked up 472 seats. The previous record was in the post-Watergate election of 1974, when Democrats picked up 628 seats. The GOP gained majorities in at least 14 state house chambers, and they now have unified control -- meaning both chambers -- of 26 state legislatures.[3]

These wins were big for the Republican Party but more importantly it was the reemergence of American conservatism that won the day. My rejection of the Democratic Party (and liberalism) in college preceded my activity in the Republican Party and the conservative movement. In Political Emancipation, I explained my personal awakenings and outlined how the Democratic Party and liberals purposely destroy the black family in order to gain political power. However, in this book I'm going in another direction.

I am proud to say that I contributed to this resurgence of conservatism by writing several articles, appearing in countless media outlets, including weekly appearances on *The Dana Show* on 97.1 FM in St. Louis speaking at Tea Party rallies, knocking on doors and finally working the polls. I believe that the outcomes of the 2010 midterm elections prove that the Tea Party movement is not a passing fad, but a political force that liberalism will have to deal with because it is here to stay.

During my travels I found no shortage of patriotism, and pure love for this country in the hearts and actions of the thousands of people. Many of these people carry constitutions, flags, and other emblems signifying their pride in being an American. Many of these people have served in the military, and even those who didn't are willing to stand and die for the ideals of our great nation.

I found during discussions with many of my fellow patriots that they have a genuine passion for improving our government, but lack the insider's understanding of our political system, how things work behind the scenes, and the role that the media plays in shaping the political landscape. Sure, most people understand that politicians should work for the people and not the other way around. They understand the three branches of government, the basics of the Constitution and a lot of the things that we were taught in civics. However, I have found through my education and my real-life work experience that there is a big difference between politics and government, and that there is another world going on behind the curtain (i.e. fundraising, polling and party dynamics.) While government is the practical functioning of the state (i.e. maintaining the roads and sewers,) politics is the art of persuading voters. You will never control the government until you understand politics.

As a student at Florida A&M University, I studied political science and history. I volunteered on Al Gore's presidential campaign (something that I'm not very proud of,) volunteered on Jeb Bush's successful gubernatorial re-election campaign, worked on several local campaigns, and interned at the Florida House of Representatives for three years.

In addition to my work in politics, I was also heavily involved in student media. I produced and hosted a television talk show for two years and wrote for the *Famuan* (campus newspaper) and *Journey Magazine* (campus magazine.) My work in student journalism prepared me for a public relations internship at Procter & Gamble, a Fortune 500 company, where I spent the entire summer learning valuable lessons on how to deal with the media and how marketing and public relations work together.

After graduating from college, I spent six years working as a District Representative for United States Senator George Voinovich. As one of Senator George Voinovich's District Representatives, I got to spend a lot of time with him. I have the utmost respect for him as a public servant and as a man. He served as a State Representative, County Commissioner, Mayor of Cleveland, Governor of Ohio and Senator. He is a generous man and shared a great deal of knowledge with me during our drives up and down Ohio's roads. His candor really helped me understand complex issues going on in the world. I worked out of the Cincinnati office where I represented the Senator in nearly 20 counties in southwestern Ohio, ranging from cities like Cincinnati and Dayton to rural communities like Greenville, Wilmington and Washington Courthouse. This experience taught me lessons in politics far beyond the scope of my textbooks. I got to take an active part of our political system and see firsthand how the federal government interacts with state and local governments, businesses, non-profits and American citizens. My duties included writing the Senator's speeches, organizing his schedule, presenting on his behalf, meeting with constituent groups, touring facilities, and even a little casework. I learned that there is a lot more to this stuff than what we see on TV.

So why is this book important? This book is important because I am using my experiences in politics and media to explain how the main stream media utilizes tenets of communism with public relations to control the minds of the people. As I explained in Political Emancipation, my life experiences growing up as a black man in America gave me a front-row seat to how liberals exploit black people. Now, I'm going to explain how liberals use the power of words and intimidation to control the entire population.

In *The Citizen's Guide To Defeating the Mainstream Media*, I discuss how contemporary politicians and the mainstream media use the same tactics as ruthless communist leaders to control people through the use of language and the cult of personality. I will also provide tools that you can use with your friends and civic groups to better improve communication and prepare you to combat false narratives that you are destined to encounter.

2010 was a great year for the Tea Party movement. Now it's time to celebrate and move on. We have to not only encourage the people we voted for to adhere to the Constitution, we have to continue to empower ourselves through knowledge and a realistic understanding of how our government and politics works. This book is designed to help you deal with the main stream media that does not have your best interests in mind.

In 2010, we also saw the rise and emergence of the citizen activist. Like many others concerned patriots, I found myself speaking at rallies, writing blog posts, and appearing on interviews. While I have years of training and experience conducting interviews, most of the patriots I've met traveling across the country have never had any media experience. All of a sudden stay-at-home moms, small business owners, blue-collar and white-collar workers that were simply concerned about the direction of our country found themselves standing behind a microphone and/or in front of a television camera.

However, the most important purpose behind this book is to create media savvy grassroots conservatives that understand the tactics of the liberal media and are equipped to combat them. The liberal establishment and the main stream media fear an informed electorate that is able to fully understand tactics that men have used to control each other for generations. Your cerebral emancipation is the biggest threat to liberal tyranny!

This book is designed to teach concerned citizens how to thrive in an often hostile media environment for conservatives. For a fraction of the cost, you are going to learn lessons that people like Jim Carville and Paul Begala charge thousands of dollars for. Make no mistake about it, learning how to deal with the media is not cheap. In the 2004 federal races, more than $1.85 billion flowed through a professional corps of consultants whose influence plays an important, though largely unexamined, role in the unrelenting escalation of campaign spending, a groundbreaking Center for Public Integrity study has found. In 2004, it took an average of $7 million to win a seat in the Senate and $1 million to win a seat in the House, an eleven-fold increase since 1976. Candidates running for Congress in 2006 spent 12 percent more overall than in 2004 according to the FEC.[4] Much of this money is spent on professional consultants that craft messages, create imagery, and personas in order to attain power. As a local candidate, I spent roughly $2000 on consulting. The costs people are willing to pay to control your mind continues to rise.

1

The Power of Propaganda

No matter where you go somebody is trying to sell you something. Some people are trying to sell you goods, others sell services, and some are trying to sell ideas. No matter what they're trying to sell you, their objective is to get something from you. Every human being is motivated by something. That motivation can be fueled by greed, power, lust, knowledge and self-righteousness, to make the world a better place or anything else. I have learned to never put boundaries on the human mind because it is capable of the most heinous atrocities and the most intimate compassion.

Perhaps I would have to say this because I have a hard time trusting people. It's not that I believe that all people are bad. I just know from study and experience that all humans are motivated by some type of personal gain. This personal gain can come from acquiring wealth or just seeking some good feeling. For example, one person may be motivated by money. He doesn't care who he hurts in the process, as long as he acquires more wealth. Another person may seek political power. He doesn't care what he has to say or how much he has to change his position in order to get elected. Another person may just want to do what he believes will help his community. He doesn't care if his actions have a detrimental effect on the people that he believes he is "helping" because he believes the things he is doing is "helping" other people regardless, if they don't want his "help." This is simply human nature.

When you understand this aspect of human nature, you realize that biases are part of human nature. The founders of the United States understood this as well. They knew that those that seek a role in government want power to control. Many conservatives seek to pursue politics in order to use its power to empower citizens to control themselves while limiting the government's reach and scope. Liberals, on the other hand, pursue politics in order to control the behavior of people.

Our founders warned of this because they understood human behavior and the nature of power. This is the basis behind the separation of powers and the limited role of government. I encourage you to understand the Federalist Papers and be familiar with it. My favorite is #51 in which James Madison explains checks and balances, human nature and the dangers of men governing men. "If men were angels, no government would be necessary. If angels were to govern men, neither external nor internal controls on government would be necessary."[5] The Founding Fathers understood the addictive nature of power.

Unfortunately, we are seeing their worst fears come to pass with the healthcare law, cap & trade, card check, the "Un"-fairness doctrine and the list goes on. In unstable countries, firearms are the weapon of choice used to seize power in government. However, in our Western civilizations, propaganda is the primary weapon of choice used to acquire power in the government. Broadly defined, propaganda is communication with the intention of manipulating opinion. Propagandists generally eschew rational argument, and their messages can assume various forms, ranging from the poisonous slur to the idealistic platitude or deliberate over-simplification.[6]

A big part of liberalism is to always portray itself as "fresh and new." They want people to believe that they are the open-minded people at the forefront of societal evolution, as opposed to Conservatives who are backwards thinking people stuck in the past. The reality is that there is nothing new about the contemporary liberals. In fact, everything they do is nothing more than putting new polish on an inoperable old car. They learn their tactics of propaganda and mind control from their heroes of the past. Liberal icons like Karl Marx, Friedrich Engels, Joseph Stalin, Woodrow Wilson and Franklin Delano Roosevelt knew how to re-package collectivism in a way that was contemporarily appealing to those who are have not studied the past and are oblivious to what's happening in the present.

Many of them used various forms of propaganda in order to control other people since the beginning of time. Primitive societies like the Mongols used strength and might to control other men. Then forms of religion were used as a basis to determine who will control the others. Then monarchies used bloodline to determine who would lead. With the evolution of man and the creation of the state, compelling speeches and effective communication was needed in order to win control of government instead of violent coups. No form of civilized government survives without the use of propaganda.

In civilized governments structures where power is determined by the electorate (i.e. Republican forms of government or John Locke's social contract,) savvy candidates become elected officials if they can tap into the discontent of the masses. During typical election cycles, there is an issue that engages society. In the cases where there is no clearly defined issue, it is up to the candidate to create one. Since the beginning of time there have always been people that have a great deal of resources at their disposal. We call them "the rich." Next are people with some resources but not an overwhelming amount - we call them the "middle class." Then there are people that are perpetually without resources and we call them "the poor." In reality, there is no way to quantify any of these categories because it is always relative. Is a single college-educated schoolteacher living in Manhattan (New York City), known for its high cost of living, making $100,000 year salary rich or poor? Is a married father of four electrician, with an Associates degree, that runs a small business with three employees making $100,000 a year in a rural community rich or poor? The answers to these questions will vary depending on who answers them.

Those who seek elected political power understand this dynamic. They understand that there are more people that are considered "middle-class" than "rich" or "poor". They understand that there are more "poor" people than there are "rich" people. They also understand that every vote counts the same regardless of income. They understand that "the poor" are too often uneducated and easily manipulated. So a savvy politician that can manipulate these numbers can use populist propaganda as a way to acquire power.

Populism is defined by the Cambridge dictionary as "political ideas and activities that are intended to represent ordinary people's needs and wishes."[7] It is used by politicians to purposely encourage people to classify themselves into separate groups. It is the basis of class warfare. In the case of the political discourse it is used to create a schism between the electorate most often pitting "the people" against "the elite", and urges social and political system changes. The use of the word "change" is at the center of populism. President Obama used this as his rallying cry during his campaign. When asked, his supporters had no clue what this meant. That is the way it is designed. I'm sure Obama knew that his campaign was built on classic communist ambiguity.

The populist propaganda that creates divisions amongst people is only effective when it is the primary weapon used by leftists in order to control other people. The left cannot stand on its ideas. Their political existence is dependent upon creating jealousy, class animosity, and people undermining their own potential by accepting labels like "disenfranchised." They believe they are unable to rise above their perceived shortcomings without a collectivist movement led by some self-appointed leader. At the same time they have to present themselves as the ones that are seeking peace and unity. This conflicting duality is a common thread of Karl Marx, Joseph Stalin, Joseph Biden, Saul Alinsky, the Democratic National Committee and any other leftist. If a day ever comes when people look in the mirror and are happy with what they see and do not measure themselves against the possessions of others, liberalism will be dead!

In the United States, President Andrew Jackson was revolutionary in his use of populist propaganda in order to organize what is considered the "common man." He organized the working class by tapping into their angst and using it to distinguish them from the elite of the day. Perhaps the elites (the Republican Party had not been founded) were growing distant from people. He seized the opportunity to acquire power in a way that no one had ever done in the country's short history. He saw that there was a desire for people to have more input in their federal government, so he mobilized people and convinced them that he knew best. He taught the unsophisticated masses to trust in his leadership and those who he endorsed. He was the Democratic Party's first demagogue. He taught his followers not to trust anyone but him. This is the same top-down model that the Democrats use today.[8]

Class warfare and jealousy have been around since the beginning of time. In the Ten Commandments, God commanded us not to covet the

21

possessions of others. He addressed jealousy. Throughout the Bible he shows us that we are all different. Some are granted more gifts and talents than others. He alone is the arbiter of these things. He expects us to do the best that we can with what we are given. Communism is the antithesis of God's word. It seeks to make everyone the same, except for the ones making the rules. With liberals we learn that some people are more equal than others.

2

New Day, Same Tactics

Karl Marx should be credited as one of the first people to really define communism and distribute it to the masses as a new way of governing. While I vehemently disagree with him on substance, I will credit his ability to articulate communism in a way that was attractive to people that consider themselves downtrodden. His doctrine purposely provided false hope that a collectivist movement led by so-called "enlightened" human beings can defy the laws of human nature.

Although the term *communism* did not come into use until the 1840s, it is derived from the Latin *communis*, meaning "shared" or "common." Visions of a society that may be considered communist appeared as long ago as the 4th century BCE.[9] It is based on the naive belief that humans will actually share all resources, forfeit all individuality and put all faith select peers who have been trusted to lead. It is assumed that the peer-leaders will never be seduced by the power entrusted to them. Yeah right! The consolidated communist leadership understand this, but they sell this collectivist vision to those that are either unwilling to pull their share of societal burden or those that understand the bounty available when convincing the masses to forfeit personal liberty and prosperity in exchange for basic needs. Communism is never accepted by people that are willing to sacrifice and excel. People that have confidence in their ability and faith in the creator to provide and direct them routinely reject collectivism.

The founders of the United States believed that the ideal system of government is when people are free to exercise personal liberty and pursue individual passion. Economist Adam Smith called this the invisible hand. It is the conjunction of the forces of self-interest, competition, and supply and demand, which he noted as being capable of allocating resources in society.[10] The antithesis of Smith's vision is the ideal state described in Plato's *Republic*, where the governing class of guardians devotes itself to serving the interests of the whole community. Because private ownership of goods would corrupt their owners by encouraging selfishness, Plato argued, the guardians must live as a large family that shares common ownership not only of material goods but also of spouses and children.[11]

Karl Marx and countryman Friedrich Engels were deeply disturbed by what they regarded as the injustices of a society divided by class. Appalled by the poverty and squalor in which ordinary workers lived and worked, he described their misery in grisly detail in *The Condition of the English Working Class* (1844). Marx and Engels maintained that all the problems (poverty, disease, and early death, etc.) that afflicted the proletariat (the industrial working class) were caused by capitalism. Their answer was to replace capitalism with communism. Under this alternative system, the major means of industrial production—such as mines, mills, factories, and railroads—would be publicly owned and operated for the benefit of all. They articulated their vision of a communist utopia in *Manifesto of the Communist Party* (1848), which they wrote at the commission of a small group of radicals called the Communist League.[12]

Marx set the foundation for class warfare propaganda used in the Russian Revolution. Communism (and contemporary American liberalism) is only effective when it creates animosity and discontent among the proletariat, which today we call it the "middle class." This is why the Democrats always make it clear that they are "fighting for the middle class." This constant distinction purposely drives a wedge through the electorate and fertilizes feelings of class envy and hopelessness. Although all Americans citizens share the same rights as described by our Constitution, the Democrats make it clear that their strategy is to divide and conquer by maintaining class distinctions. While leftists use class warfare propaganda as a rallying call to bring about "fairness", in actuality it is a massive power grab achieved on the backs of the trusting masses.

One thing that propaganda profiteers hate is when their targets start to receive information from other sources. The established media sources (the network television companies and the major newspapers) have been suffering financially for quite some time. Figures released in April of 2010 by the Audit Bureau of Circulations showed average weekday circulation fell 8.7 percent in the six months that ended March 31, 2010, compared with the same period a year earlier. From April through September of 2009, average weekday circulation dropped 10.6 percent and Sunday circulation fell 7.5 percent.

The top 25 newspapers in the country showed some huge losses led by The San Francisco Chronicle's weekday circulation dropping nearly 23 percent from 2009 to 241,330.[13] One of my favorite reads, The Wall Street Journal is the exception and not the rule when it comes to dying legacy news sources. It surpassed USA Today as the newspaper with the biggest U.S. circulation. In the report, the Journal once again posted the only gain in circulation among the top 25 newspapers that had comparable figures from the prior year. It grew its circulation 0.5 percent to 2.09 million.[14]

The experts like to blame the "new media" for the loss of consumers of legacy media instead of placing the blame where it really belongs. They insult the intelligence of the reader with predictable liberal bias and tired narratives. With so many alternatives including cable news, the Internet, and talk radio, former media giants no longer have a monopoly on the flow of information. The loss of this monopoly has had a major affect not only on their profitability, but their ability to control the political dialogue and the electoral process. For generations these established media sources maintained a fruitful alliance with liberal politicians and the Democratic Party. With the demise of the fairness doctrine in 1987, a new era of information began.

The Fairness Doctrine was started by the FCC in 1949 to regulate the airwaves. The rule eventually became to "afford reasonable opportunity for discussion of contrasting points of view on controversial matters of public importance." Of course the fairness doctrine was intended to be anything but "fair." It was designed by elite political operatives to suppress political opposition in the budding radio era. Bill Ruder, Democratic campaign strategist and Assistant Secretary of Commerce in the Kennedy Administration said it best when he said "Our massive strategy was to use the Fairness Doctrine to challenge and harass right-wing broadcasters and hope the challenges would be so costly to them that they would be inhibited and decide it was too expensive to continue."[15]

The death of the Fairness Doctrine in 1987 led to Rush Limbaugh and the proliferation of talk radio, as a viable source of information and profitability. Many believe that talk radio played a key role in the

Republican Revolution in 1994. Until then, the Democrats had controlled the Congress, and the Republicans had not held the majority in the House for forty years since the 83rd Congress (1952). During the midterm elections of 1994, the Republicans won a net gain of 54 seats in the House of Representatives, and a pickup of eight seats in the Senate. The gains in seats in the mid-term election resulted in the Republicans gaining control of both the House and the Senate in January 1995. Large Republican gains were made in state houses, as well, when the GOP picked up 12 gubernatorial seats and 472 legislative seats. In so doing, it took control of 20 state legislatures from the Democrats. Prior to this, Republicans had not held the majority of governorships since 1972. This was also the first time in 50 years that the GOP controlled a majority of state legislatures.[16]

There is no denying that talk radio, the Internet, blogs, and YouTube what many have called the "new media," have changed the political dialogue and how information is controlled. Their affect on elections has proven that the information monopoly is over. While this may sound like good news to you, it has proven to be bad news for many people, particularly some liberals and members of the Democratic Party. Before the new media, they were used to making statements and having their friends in the media help control the dialogue. With limited sources of information, citizens were hard pressed to find other sources to contrast what they were being told. While Democrats and liberal politicians still enjoy this advantage, it is not as prominent as it once was because citizens have other ways to check the validity of their claims.

Make no mistake about it, today's Democrat leaders and liberal activists understand the power of propaganda and controlling the flow of information. Although they claim to be the advocates of free speech, their actions and proposed legislation are the complete opposite. Saul Alinksy

27

taught in *Rules For Radicals* that in order for leftist propaganda to be effective you have to create an enemy. Proponents have to create a personification of an enemy for the masses to hate. In George Orwell's classic novel *1984,* Emmanuel Goldstein played this role. The ruling party used him to represent the biggest threat to society even though his existence was questionable. Today, Fox News is one of the left's favorite targets.

Powerful Democratic senator, Jay Rockefeller, blamed the cable news network (along with MSNBC) for creating a "politically toxic climate in Washington" and expressed his desire to see the Federal Communications Commission shut down Fox News and MSNBC. I suppose there were generations of political harmony until the advent of Fox News in 1996. "I'm tired of the right and the left," Rockefeller said during a Senate hearing on retransmission consent. "There's a little bug inside of me which wants to get the FCC to say to Fox and to MSNBC, Out. Off. End. Goodbye."[17] "It would be a big favor to political discourse; to our ability to do our work here in Congress; and to the American people, to be able to talk with each other and have some faith in their government and, more importantly, in their future," said the Rockefeller, also chairman of the Senate Committee on Commerce, Science, and Transportation.[18] The genius Rockefeller didn't seem to realize that the FCC only regulates broadcast airwaves, not cable.

Although Rockefeller may not understand the rules that govern cable news, he does understand the power of controlling people through the influence of media. He is also aware of the reach of Fox News and it's ability to challenge liberal narratives. That's why he wants to bring back the old days with only the three major networks (ABC, NBC and CBS.) There was a time when most Americans started their day by reading the newspaper, then worked all day and finally came home to receive their information from the evening news. With our 24/7 media cycle, smart phones, websites and cable news, information is spread as it happens. People like Rockefeller must envy liberal icons like Joseph Stalin because they controlled the media and the flow of information, which made it easy to control the behavior of the masses.

After electoral losses of epic proportions in 2010, Democrat leaders were left to figure out what happened and how to correct it. Instead of trying to identify why the American electorate didn't embrace their leftist policies, they concluded that the reason behind their losses was that the ungrateful masses didn't realize that the Democratic Party knows what is best for them. In the Liberals mind, people must be holding onto the foolish idea that they know what was best for their own individual lives.

As a result of the losses, Senate Majority Leader Harry Reid assigned New York Sen. Chuck Schumer the role of chief propagandist in the Senate. In a letter obtained by POLITICO, Reid told his Democrat colleagues that the party needs to "better integrate our legislative and message crafting functions into a coordinated nucleus managing policy, press and politics."[19] In layman's terms, he's saying that they have to step up their propaganda game because what they're doing is not working. He recognizes that Schumer has the gift of manipulating people, and to Democrats that's obviously more valuable than being able to craft legislation that will improve the country. "I have asked Senator Schumer, whose communications abilities and tactical skills we all greatly respect, to lead this effort as chairman of the new office."[20]

No one should be surprised that the strategy to reverse the trend of electoral losses is to focus on mind control of the masses through propaganda instead of trying to defeat the Republicans in the arena of ideas. The entire basis of liberalism revolves around convincing the masses to compromise their individual liberty in exchange for perceived safety from the state. When individuals forfeit personal power, it is transferred to the leaders of the state. The elites like Reid and Schumer use propaganda to control this power, consolidate it and divide it amongst the other members of the ruling class. This model is at the core of leftist ideology and is the antithesis of vision the Founding Fathers had of the United States of America.

President Obama also understands how dangerous it is for citizens to have too many sources of information available to them. He made a statement that "information becomes a distraction" in a speech in front of a nearly all African-American audience at the commencement of Hampton University.[21] Let's think about this. First of all, I have never been told by a teacher or boss that I did too much research or that I found too much information in order to make the most informed decision. Granted, there will always be information that may not be needed, but it's better to discard information than be oblivious of it! You will severely handicap your ability should you decide to follow the president's advice of limiting the amount of information gathered. It also makes me question why the president made these remarks in front of a group of intelligent African-American college graduates. There is no way that you can convince me that he would have made the same remarks in front of a group of predominantly white Ivy League graduates. I believe that the president has a disconnect with graduates of historically black colleges and universities (HBCUs) and our abilities to compete against those, like him, who were graduates of Ivy League institutions in the same manner that he doesn't believe Justice Clarence Thomas is as intelligent as the white members of the Supreme Court.

The true motivation behind the president's comments is not just his disconnect with graduates of HBCUs, but his desire to reinforce the notion to the Democrat's most loyal voting bloc, that they should depend on him and his party for guidance (political and otherwise). There is no need for us to have to worry about considering any other points of view. He is assuring us that we have the luxury of him guiding us (black folks) so that we can spend our time doing other things like worshiping him or being entertained. We should leave the politics to the Ivy Leaguers like him.

I lost a tremendous amount of respect for then-candidate Obama, after his comments were directed at Justice Clarence Thomas. During a prominent candidate forum he stated that he would not have nominated Clarence Thomas to the Supreme Court. Duh! Anyone with an ounce of brain tissue would know that the likelihood of a contemporary Democrat president nominating any constitutional conservative to the Supreme Court is far-fetched at best. I get that. "I would not have nominated Clarence Thomas," said Obama. "I don't think that he..." the crowd interrupted with applause. "I don't think that he was a strong enough jurist or legal thinker at the time for that elevation. Setting aside the fact that I profoundly disagree with his interpretations of a lot of the constitution. I would not have nominated Justice Scalia though I don't think there is any doubt about his intellectual brilliance. Because he and I just disagree."[22]

The problem that I have was his vicious assault on the intelligence of the only black man on the court yet praising white member's judicial aptitude, and even recognizing his philosophical disagreement with them. This is black on black crime in it's highest form. Obama has shown through his actions, not his rhetoric, how he really feels about black people in America. When I say black, I don't mean him. He is literally an African-American. Black American is the culture experienced by people like me who are descendents of slaves. An experience that he has no clue about. I believe that he has a fundamental disconnect with black people in this country because he doesn't share our heritage. He is the benefactor of our struggle, but has no biological or cultural connection to us. Therefore, he looks at us as political tools like the rest of his liberal elitist cohorts. We are a naive and necessary voting bloc to him. His absence in the black community was clearly visible until he started to campaign to us days before the mid-term election of 2010. The President ignored black folks for the better part of two years, and then expected us to not only vote for his comrades, but to do endless campaign work as well. It doesn't matter if it is condemning inner-city black children to failing schools[23], insulting the intelligence of a black Supreme Court justice or cutting funding from HBCUs[24], Obama has proven that when it comes to African-Americans, he can talk the talk, but not walk the walk.

3

Recognizing Main Stream Media Tactics

Ambiguity

Perhaps the most frustrating part of American politics is ambiguity. It is described as "doubtfulness or uncertainty of meaning or intention." In plain language, it is the ability to answer a question without answering the question. It's a true sign of one's mastery of language, and more art than science. A master politician can use this art form to wiggle out of the tightest squeeze. While many casual political observers may indeed grow frustrated with a politician's inability to take a concrete position on controversial issues, citizens need to understand it's place in our American culture.

Our founding fathers believed that ambiguity was a necessary component in the creation of our republic and key ingredient for it's survival. While our Constitution's language is explicit in some regards, it is also purposely vague in others. It was designed to possess concrete (inalienable) rights. It also provides future generations the opportunity to make adjustments. Edward H. Levy probably best describes this dynamic in his book <u>An Introduction to Legal Reasoning</u>. He states:

In an important sense legal rules are never clear, and, if a rule had to be clear before it could be imposed, society would be impossible. The mechanism accepts the differences of view and ambiguities of words. It provides the participation of the community in resolving the ambiguity by providing a forum for the discussion of policy in the gap of ambiguity. On serious controversial questions, it makes it possible to take the first step in the direction of what otherwise would be forbidden ends. The mechanism is indispensable to peace in the community.[25]

Doublethink

Having spent years studying politics, history, and language, I find it fascinating that the media is able to convince people to believe conflicting narratives. The creation and perpetuation of these contradictory beliefs cannot be possible without a media structure, as well as educational structure that discourages and too often scorns analytical thinking. In George Orwell's novel "1984", he described this as "doublethink" which is the power to hold two completely contradictory beliefs in one's mind simultaneously, and accept both of them.

Understanding "doublethink" and the process of creating conflicting narratives will help you navigate through the political word games. Liberals and the media have figured out that injecting emotion into rational debate confuses those who cannot separate fact from feelings. The liberal elite have used this tactic to control black people by using powerful accusations like racism, bigotry, and injustice that conjure up fierce emotions yet are nearly impossible to define. You will notice that the biggest supporters of liberalism too often can't define this doctrine or the policies that result from it. This lack of critical thinking and intellectual maturity is why liberals prey on those in hardship, those with little education, particularly the so-called poor, children and students.

Taking advantage of the homeless and drug abusers was a big part of Obama's election strategy.[26]

I got a message from moveon.org bragging about how productive the Democrat-controlled Congress (2009-2011) had been by passing Obamacare, the stimulus bills and financial reform. For years, Democrats told us how great these things would be. However, once they became law, many Democrat supporters ran as far away from these "accomplishments" as they could, while others campaigned against them. When the polls began to show that the Democrats were facing an electoral tsunami, their strategy was to not only run away from their record, but to double down on confusing voters.

Although the Democrats had nearly two years of a supermajority and were able to pass major legislation, many incumbent Democrats didn't run on their record. They spent millions of dollars on a barrage of the most vicious attack ads in the history of politics. Of course, the media didn't hold liberals accountable. Instead, it did it's best to accommodate the attacks and assist in the attacks. In an apparent accidental voice mail message left on the cell phone of Joe Miller's spokesperson, Randy DeSoto, who is believed to be the news director for CBS Anchorage affiliate KTVA, was talking with assignment editor Nick McDermott and other reporters, openly discuss creating, if not fabricating, two stories about Republican nominee for U.S. Senate, Joe Miller.[27] During the discussion one reporter said "We know that out of all the people that will show up tonight, at least one of them will be a registered sex offender." In order to cover up their intentions to sink Miller's campaign, the CBS affiliate released a statement saying that the "The group of KTVA news personnel was reviewing potential "what-if" scenarios, discussing the likelihood of events at the rally and how KTVA might logistically disseminate any breaking news."[28]

When researching and deciding positions on political issues, it's best to remove all personal bias and seek facts in order to make informed decisions. Unfortunately, this could be a challenge because we no longer live in a country where the media reports the news. The mainstream media has drawn a line in the sand and clearly shown us what side of the line they're on. They continue to move further to the left.

Positioning

Another key lesson I learned while working in journalism was that what's *not* reported is just as powerful as what *is* reported. When you listen to conservative talk radio, you often hear callers and hosts talking about the double standard in the media. They talk about how the media pounces all over transgressions by conservatives while virtually ignoring transgressions by liberals.

Positioning the story has a great deal to do with its impact. When the media wants a story to be major they will constantly lead with it. This means the story will be on the front page of the newspaper with several pages and stories supporting it. The stories are located in the places where readers are most likely to read it. On television, the stories are the first reported, have the most time dedicated to it, and are often referred to several times during the course of the program. These tactics are used when they want the story to be big. On the other hand when they want something to go away they either don't report it at all or give it very little attention. They used to be able to get away with this before the advent of conservative talk radio, the Internet and the new media.

Kelly Williams-Bolar, an Ohio mother of two, made national news when she was sentenced to 10 days in jail and placed on three years probation after sending her kids to a school district in which they did not live.

Although she lived in an Akron housing project, she used her father's address in nearby Copley Township so that her children could attend a better school district. This is against the law. The media immediately began to position the story as the ongoing persistence of racial prejudice in the judicial system and society. Liberal activist Dr. Boyce Watkins commented "This case is also an example of how racial-inequality created during slavery and Jim Crow continues to cripple our nation to this day. There is no logical reason on earth why this mother of two should be dehumanized by going to jail and be left permanently marginalized from future economic and educational opportunities. Even if you believe in the laws that keep poor kids trapped in underperforming schools, the idea that this woman should be sent to jail for demanding educational access is simply ridiculous." [29]

This is the typical narrative that the media loves to perpetuate. What the mainstream media and Dr. Boyce Watkins failed to mention is why was this mother forced to take such drastic measures? The reality is, the ones that believe in what she calls "laws that keep poor kids trapped in underperforming schools" are the liberal politicians and labor unions that he defends. Dr. Watkins, a fierce Obama supporter, and the media purposely omit the role of the teacher's unions and liberal opposition to school choice programs. In fact, they purposely confuse the issue by conjuring images of Jim Crow, slavery, and any other types of incendiary language instead of acknowledging that this situation is the direct result of parents lack of educational choices. In cases like this, where the blood is clearly on the hands of liberal legislators, the media will focus on the symptoms instead of the solution because the genesis of this problem points directly at liberals. They will use this as an opportunity to advance their racial and class warfare narratives instead acknowledging that the reason why concerned parents like Williams-Bolar resort to desperate measures is because liberals like Dr. Boyce Watkins and President

Obama purposely fight to keep her kids in failing schools by prioritizing union bosses over parents.

One of Obama's first acts as president was to ensure that stories like this become commonplace. The president signed the $410 billion dollar omnibus spending bill for fiscal year 2009. It included a provision that lets funding for the Washington D.C.'s school voucher program to expire at the end of the 2010 school year. The program allowed about 1,700 mostly low-income and minority students to attend private schools as an alterative to the struggling D.C. public school system. Press Secretary Robert Gibbs said "The president doesn't believe that vouchers are a long-term answer to our educational problems and the challenges that face our public school system, where the vast majority of students are educated in this country." [30] In other words, Obama doesn't care if parents like Kelly Williams-Bolar have to go to jail in order to have some kind of control over where their kid goes to school, as long as his union boss friends are happy. Democrats have proven time and time again that African-American concerns are never a priority because they will suffer no political backlash. Blacks have proven to be very politically predictable and will not hold them accountable. Therefore Democrats are empowered to use their political capital to appease other supporters. Do you really think that black parents going to jail and black kids condemned to failing schools will cause blacks to stop voting Democrat?

In true liberal sleight-of-hand fashion, after doing everything in his power to put parents like Williams-Bolar in desperate situations, Obama tries to use this opportunity to look like a hero. On his Change.Org website he is trying to pressure Ohio Republican Gov. John Kasich to pardon Mrs. Williams-Bolar. [31] The liberals will use this as another opportunity to make Republicans look like racists while the entire situation is a direct result of liberal determination to keep educational choices out of the hands of low income parents. Conservatives need to be aware of how the media is going to shape this. They will never address the real reason which is the powerful unions and liberals whose existence depends on blacks staying poor and uneducated.

Shaping data

Politicians love to say "you're entitled to your own opinions, but you're not entitled to your own facts." This may be true, but what they don't mention is that you can shape facts and statistics to validate your opinion. It's real easy to take data and shape it to support your premise. You do this by controlling who gets surveyed and how you frame the questions and results. For instance, the way the media reports presidential approval ratings is easily skewed.

It is customary to poll job approval and job disapproval at the same time using a series of different questions. Let's say you have two different presidents. Both have a job disapproval rating of 40% and a job approval rating of 45%. One favored is by the media and the other one is not. When the media reports about the president it doesn't like, they will lead their stories with headlines like "The President's job disapproval rating reaches another low at 40%" or "only 45% of Americans approve of the job of the President." However, when they report results on the favorable president you'll see headlines like "Nearly half of all Americans approve of the job of the President" or "Only 40% of Americans disapprove the job of the President." Certain words can be used to make the same numbers look harsh or impressive. Journalists can use the power of language to present a point of view in order to persuade the thoughts of the reader.

Coded Messages

Politics is not only a game of language, it is a game of illusion. It's no different than Harry Houdini performing magic. A master politician, just like a master magician, has the ability to make people see things that aren't there and to make people believe that fiction is real. Politicians use the media as a platform to send out messages to their political base, party leadership, and the general public. Coded messages make statements that speak to the issue at hand while remaining noticeably vague. The purpose is to be able to use the same language to communicate to different people, because people interpret things differently based on their knowledge of subject, concern, and emotional attachment. Master politicians know this.

Let's examine a few statements from politicians and how they could be interpreted by different people:

I am committed to building an economic approach that lifts every American, not just the privileged few. The average American CEO earns more before lunchtime in one day than a minimum wage worker earns all year.[32]
Rep. Nancy Pelosi

Liberal: She is supportive of labor unions. She will fight to make sure the rich pay their fair share of taxes.
Conservative: This is class warfare in its purest form. This is a declaration of war on success.
Casual observer: She is fighting to make sure that the economy is fair for everyone.

Sen. Jim DeMint believes that strong families are the true strength of America. That's why it is so important that our nation protect the lives of the most vulnerable, the unborn, and encourage loving families that choose to adopt children in need of a home. That's why we must protect marriage between a man and a woman because we know children that are raised by a mother and father have the best chance to succeed.[33]

Sen. Jim DeMint

Liberal: He wants to take control from mothers and abolish abortion. He is going to fight to make sure that homosexuals don't enjoy the same rights as everyone else like adoption and marriage.

Conservative: He is fighting to preserve our American family values. He believes that slaughtering unborn babies is reprehensible.

Casual observer: He wants to make sure that children grow up in a safe and loving environment.

The Mainstream Media Echo Chamber

The term "media echo chamber" can refer to any situation in which information, ideas or beliefs are amplified or reinforced by transmission inside an "enclosed" space. Observers of journalism in the mass media describe an echo chamber effect in media discourse.[34] Liberals use the echo chamber to either demonize conservatives or close ranks to protect liberal interests. They also use it to smear (repeat intentionally false or misleading information) conservatives. Today it's much easier to start a misinformation campaign. The media can now blame some obscure blog for starting a baseless accusation and then run with information without taking any responsibility.

It starts when some influential liberal sets the marching orders. The accusations then circulates throughout the Internet. Then liberal thought leaders, media figures, celebrities and politicians began to endlessly recite the same talking points. The point is to assault the general public with the endless barrage of repetitious statements in order to pound their brains into submission. The desired goal is to force them into seeing things their way. It doesn't matter if it's true or false. They have a narrative to maintain and a job to do. Leftist icon, Vladimir Lenin, describes the contemporary mainstream media echo chamber the best stating, "A lie told often enough becomes the truth."[35]

The overall effect often is to legitimize false claims in the public eye, through sheer volume of reporting and media references, even if the majority of these reports acknowledge the original factual inaccuracy of the story. Even if they print a correction (which are never prominently featured), the damage has already been done. In the not too distant past, journalists had integrity. They would actually check their sources before taking anything to print because their reputation was on the line. Their reputations used to have value. Many in today's mainstream media have no integrity, so it's easy for them to spread lies.

The person that best captures examples of the media echo chamber is Rush Limbaugh. Rush captures the liberal echo chamber in his frequent media montages. He takes clips from top mainstream media figures and puts together a string of quotes proving how pervasive and redundant the echo chamber is.

In July of 2010, the media was trying to convince the American public that "Obama Brought the Economy Back from the Brink." I suppose their goal was for us to ignore the escalating unemployment, the lack of job creation, and watching our neighbors lose their homes. Their real goal was to protect Obama and the Democrats leading into the 2010 midterm elections.

RUSH: Folks, we've put together a montage here. Changing gears here now because we're going to get to your phone calls after the break coming up and the other items here in the Stack of Stuff, but I have been noticing throughout the ruling class media, the phrase "Obama brought us back from the brink." It would have been far worse had it not been for Obama. Obama brought us back from the brink. Here is -- and it's a lie -- a montage of ruling class media types since last Wednesday.

HARRIS: It seems so long ago that the economy was literally on the brink.

CLIFT: (crosstalk) He brought the economy back from the brink.

KEILAR: Two years ago the U.S. economy being on the brink of collapse.

HARWOOD: Helped pull the economy back from the brink.

MENENDEZ: He has managed to get a lot done, saving the economy from the brink.

LOTHIAN: As the President has pointed out it's been brought back from the brink.

CARLSON: Obama having to regulate the banks, after the banks put all of us on the brink of a economic collapse.

RUSH: By the way, remember the montage we had of the media talking about gravitas, Bush needing to select Cheney to have gravitas on the ticket? They think the same; they act the same; they speak the same; it's required to be in the ruling class. So here now is another incarnation of this. Obama brought us back from the brink. The next time you hear that, the next time you hear Obama brought us back from the brink, ask yourself, "Why can't he get us over the hump?"[36]

The best way to counter the mainstream media tactics is to first understand them. Learn how to recognize them so that you can take control over your own thoughts because their goal is to take control of your thoughts so that you will act and behave in the way that they want you to behave. By recognizing their tactics, understanding their goal, cross referencing the facts, and researching you will become powerful. Although rejecting their mind control will certainly make you unpopular among liberals and could subject you to their wrath. However, owning your mind is worth the sacrifice.

4

Countering Liberal Narratives

The contemporary American media operates using several predictable templates in order to control the flow of information to the American public. One thing I learned as a staff writer for the student run newspaper (*The FAMUAN*) and as a TV personality while in college was that sentence structure or tone could drastically change the context. For example:

I will cut your taxes
I **will** cut your taxes
I will **cut** your taxes
I will cut **your** taxes

This same sentence could have four different interpretations.

I will cut your taxes- Emphasizing the word "I" could be interpreted as the speaker taking charge and assuming responsibility of the task of cutting taxes.
I **will** cut your taxes- emphasizing the word "will" could be interpreted as the speaker making a promise.
I will **cut** your taxes- Emphasizing the word "cut" could be interpreted as the speaker accepting a monumental task on your behalf.

I will cut **your** taxes- emphasizing the word "your" could be interpreted as a speaker taking a special interest to personally serve you and/or your constituency.

I believe that many people underestimate the power of communication. There are many assumptions made when consuming information from the mainstream media. Perhaps the most basic assumption is that the information presented is factual and unbiased. The reader also assumes that the news stories are presented with integrity. Unfortunately this is no longer the case with the American political media. Having been both a news writer and an opinion writer, I know that people write from their perspective. It's natural. Although I only worked in a newsroom as an collegian, I know several friends that became professional news writers. When we have candid conversations about liberal media bias they all agreed that it is not a myth.

Many conservatives are certain that there is a liberal bias in most newsrooms across the country. Some may believe that this bias is based on a concerted effort to advance the liberal agenda. I believe that this bias is used to promote the agenda of liberalism because the people that gravitate towards this profession overwhelmingly tend to be liberally minded. Not only do an overwhelming majority of writers have liberal philosophies, they are also heavy donors to the Democratic Party. Regardless of the reason, the fact is that people with liberal philosophies are reporting the news. You'd have to be naïve to think that they would never use their expertise, platform and mastery of language to position the Democrats in a favorable light, and at the same time position the Republicans unfavorably.

Some news organizations may prohibit their journalists from donating to political candidates and causes, but many journalists still donate.[37] Some may argue that it is inconsequential whether or not journalists donate to politicians and political causes. They will insist that a professional journalist would never inject bias into his work. "Despite the potential for controversy, some journalists who've made political contributions reject the notion that their interests are conflicting, saying their action as private citizens and as journalists are not mutually exclusive," OpenSecrets.org reported.[38] I suppose a fool would believe that someone would donate hundreds if not thousands of dollars to support a candidate and not care about the outcome. However, in the United States that's not the case.

In 2007, Bill Dedman at MSNBC did a massive research project examining political donations by journalists over several years and found a similar overwhelming number of Democratic journalists (125 of 143 political donors) gave to Democratic candidates while only 16 gave to Republican candidates.[39] In 2008, William Tate wrote in Investors Business Daily that 235 journalists donated to Democrats while only 20 gave to Republicans for a total of $225,563 to Democrats and $16,298 to Republicans.[40] While that may seem insignificant to the over $1 billion collected during that election cycle, it's enough to prove that journalists had a stake in the outcome of the election. Keep in mind that these are only the journalists bold enough to go on record as donors. I am sure there are others that showed allegiance to the Democratic Party through in-kind donations (perhaps their work.)

The mainstream media's financial stake in the 2008 presidential election turned out to be quite an advantage for Barack Obama over rival John McCain. It just so happens that the coverage of Obama was somewhat more positive than negative, but not markedly so. The big difference was that the coverage of McCain has been heavily unfavorable and it only got worse as the election got closer. The Pew Research Center's Project for

Excellence in Journalism reported that in the six weeks following the conventions through the final debate, unfavorable stories about McCain outweighed favorable ones by a factor of more than three-to-one -- the most unfavorable of all four candidates. For Obama during this period, just over a third of the stories were clearly positive in tone (36%), while a similar number (35%) were neutral or mixed. A smaller number (29%) were negative. For McCain, by comparison, nearly six-in-ten stories studied were decidedly negative in nature (57%), while fewer than two-in-ten (14%) were positive.[41]

The 2010 midterm elections was no different in regard to journalists having a financial stake in the outcome of the election. Analysis by the Center for Responsive Politics (CRP) found that 235 self-identified U.S. journalists or news organization employees "donated more than $469,900 to federal political candidates, committees and parties during the 2010 election." OpenSecrets.org noted that "the median amount" of donations was $500 and that more money went to Democrats (65%) than Republicans. And six "media professionals" gave "more than five figures since January 2009," including Vogue's editor Anna Wintour, who gave $30,400 to the Democratic National Convention, the maximum contribution.[42]

One of the main reasons why people are turning away from the mainstream media is because of its predictability. The media continues to use some of the same flawed narratives that people can no longer accept as the truth. People now have the ability and means to fact check and challenge the assertions from the mainstream media. The following are some of the typical liberal narratives with solutions to counter them.

Topic: Voting

Liberal Narrative: All black people are Democrats

Perhaps the liberal narrative that infuriates me the most is the notion that blacks, particularly their loyalty, is property of the Democratic Party. When I tell black people that I'm a registered Republican, I'm always asked the same stupid question, "why are you a Republican?" Many black people that consider themselves Republicans answer this differently. Some say that it is important for black people to be represented in both parties. Some say that blacks were originally loyal to the Republican Party. Some say that their personal ideology aligns more with Republicans. That's fine for them, but I don't answer it that way.

Whenever I am asked this asinine question I reply "because I can. I was born free and I'm free to support whoever I want." If I'm in the mood for discussion, I may follow up with "why are you a Democrat?" The fact is the Democratic Party is the party of slavery, is the party of Jim Crow, is the party that supports policies that continue to wreak havoc on our communities by producing poverty, broken families and perpetual educational failure. I also say that I am not property of the Democrat party. Furthermore I have no problem articulating why I am a Republican while so many black people cant answer any questions about the history, platform or their reasons for undying support of the Democrats. My birth certificate states my name, Palm Beach County and the state of Florida. Unlike some people, I don't mind showing it. Nowhere on my birth certificate does it say "property of the Democratic Party" or "is condemned to blindly obey liberal orthodoxy for the rest of his life." Its time liberals acknowledge that forcefully making people make choices against their will because of their birth race is called slavery. Like every other American, I am free to be apart of any group I choose and, therefore, I don't go into any further explanation.

Furthermore, the question is based on an inherently flawed premise. Once again it goes back to the power of language. The premise of the question is the assumption that being a Republican is contrary to being black. It makes the assumption that blacks should be Democrats and therefore blacks that are not are betraying their race. For this reason I don't consider myself a "black Republican" or a "black conservative." I am a Republican or a conservative. Blacks don't consider themselves "black Democrats" or "black liberals" because they assume that to be black is to be a Democrat and to be black is to be liberal. Both assumptions are narratives that have been perpetuated for several generations now and have been implanted into the psyche of the contemporary black American. Supporting Democratic candidates is now a reflex for black Americans and not a choice.

Carter G. Woodson described the liberal control of black Democrats when he said "When you control a man's thinking you do not have to worry about his actions. You do not have to tell him not to stand here or go yonder. He will find his 'proper place' and will stay in it. You do not need to send him to the back door. He will go without being told. In fact, if there is no back door, he will cut one for his special benefit. His education makes it necessary."[43]

The liberal narrative contends that black Republicans are sellouts to the black community. No matter how much a black Republican tries to "prove his blackness" by telling people how much Jay-Z he listens to, or how tough the project complex he up grew in was, or the quality of education he received from a historically black college, he still is going to be cast as a sellout because he doesn't buy into the liberal agenda. With this understanding I don't try to defend my beliefs because they are going to stick to their narrative anyway. If you seek to convert someone's thinking, it's best to find people willing to entertain different points of view. It's a fool's errand to try to convert a victim of brainwashing.

Ideas to counter it:
The way you combat this narrative is honesty. Make liberals explain why they believe that when black babies are born they should have to unconditionally obey the policy directives of the Democratic Party for the rest of their lives. Ask why blacks that disagree with liberal policies should be interrogated. Make them cite sources from the Bible, their political charter, the African-American birth charter or some other place that outlines why blacks are held to a different political standard than Hispanics, Asians or Whites. Don't even make it about policy. Continue to profess that you believe that every American, regardless of their race, is entitled to make any political decisions they choose. Make them defend why black people in particular should be loyal to the Democratic Party (regardless of what policies they pursue) for their entire lives. Make them explain why blacks that don't support the Democratic Party should be subject to insults and rejection from their own community.

This is an opportunity where you can contrast conservative versus liberal values. Liberals, by nature, group people and believe that they own black people's minds and votes. On the other hand conservatives believe that people are entitled to make the decisions that best reflect their desires. Of course, liberals will never admit that they believe that they own black people. This is where you must focus on the facts and make them defend their position. Be ready to explain why you believe that all people are free to make their own choices.

Topic: Poverty

Liberal Narrative: Conservatives want people to live in poverty

One of the best ways that liberals control people is through the exploitation of poverty. Liberals use poverty as a weapon against conservative policies. The media narrative dictates that only liberals care about and seek to protect the impoverished, while conservatives hate this group of people and want them all to starve and live in the cold. Nothing could be further from the truth. The fact is liberals depend on the so-called "impoverished" people because they provide a great deal of uncontested votes. These people typically don't value education in the same manner as others in society. Therefore liberals know that they are easily controlled.

Who is easier to control, a hungry man or a confident man? The answer is a hungry man. The liberals understand this. When a liberal campaigns to a hungry man he tells him that he will provide enough for him and his children to survive until things get better (purposely indefinite.) He taps into his angst in order to persuade him to personify an enemy and blame him for his perceived misfortune. In exchange, the hungry man is expected to give his vote to the liberal. From his perspective it is a small sacrifice in exchange for his children to have enough to make it through an indefinite rough time. I would imagine that initially the hungry man considers the actions of the liberal as compassionate and perhaps doesn't see himself becoming addicted to his offerings, much less it becoming a way of life. However, humans are creatures of habit. When we get used to doing things and having things a certain way we get accustomed to it. We then resist any change to this routine. This is when liberals charter buses, load all of their victims (I mean supporters) in them, distribute signs, line them up in front of the cameras at the state capital and then watch the election results pour in. This is the basis of the liberal control of the "little guy" and what sustains their oligarchy.

Liberals have a perfect understanding of this dynamic. This is why they fought so hard to continue to expand unemployment benefits during the lame-duck compromise of 2010. Vice-President Joe Biden, in defending the extension of unemployment, stated that the president chose to "compromise to save people who are drowning." Biden told to NBC's David Gregory. "There's people out there drowning. There are two million people this month that can't afford to go get a Christmas tree, let alone buy any gifts, because their unemployment has run out...." [44] Nothing in their agenda is about empowering people. Their existence is dependent upon people not having enough intestinal fortitude to withstand difficult times and to look to the liberals for survival. Sometimes in life we have to go without things especially when times are tough. The most successful people are the ones that make sacrifices and persevere with the belief that things, will get better. People in this country survived long before government handouts.

Ideas to counter it: Self-confidence, faith in yourself and faith in a higher power is the way to combat liberal political power that is dependent upon misfortune. Let's consider the plight of a confident man. When a confident man is faced with adversity he reacts differently than the hungry man. He rejects the pittance offered by the liberal because his pride won't allow it. Even in the face of job loss or severe life changes, he understands that his trust in God and the abilities given to him will see him through. The situation may call for a downsizing of the lifestyle he had been accustomed to. This may mean that he may have to move his family to a smaller location. Although he may be used to managing hundreds of people, his pride won't prevent him from sweeping floors or making hamburgers if that's what is necessary to provide for his family. He explains to his family that these next few months or years could be difficult. At the same time his faith and his creator strengthens him because he understands that God provides in the best and worst of times. He continues to put his faith in God and not the government. So regardless of how bad the economy gets, he looks in the mirror each day and realizes that he will continue to trust his creator and his creator will provide enough within his will.

Topic: Class Warfare
Liberal Narrative: It's the government's responsibility to close the income gap

The liberal tactic of class warfare is pitting citizens against each other because of their assumed income and acquired wealth. Liberals like to cite the income gap as a reason to redistribute wealth. They use their desire to bring "fairness" to the system as a reason to use the heavy hand of government to confiscate the wealth of select citizens. The goal of fairness is ambiguous by design. Since few of them have the guts (like the Communist Party USA) to admit that they would like to transform the United States into a socialist nation, they have to mask their intentions under the guise of "fairness." On their website its states that "But to win a better life for working families, we believe that we must go further. We believe that the American people can replace capitalism with a system that puts people before profit - socialism."[45] When engaging liberals, try to get them to explain their desire in practical terms. Get them to explain their goal and then work backwards.

Ask them if they would like for all people to make the same income? Would they like for every organization to have union style pay grades? Would they like the CEO to make the same as the janitor? Would they like to get rid of pensions so when everyone retires they have the same amount of money to live off of? Perhaps they would like every citizen to make the same amount of money, so that when a medical students who sacrifices years of resources, fun, and time graduates and makes the

54

identical salary of a high school dropout that serves food in the hospital dining facility. Make them offer concrete solutions and not rhetoric. If equal income is what they want, then this is communism. This is the same style of government described by Karl Marx and implemented by Lenin and Stalin.

Wealth gap studies are a big tool used by leftists in order to convince the electorate that economic policies that emphasize redistribution of wealth should be adopted by the United States government. For instance, a study by the Institute on Assets and Social Policy at Brandeis University found that the Black-White wealth Gap is growing. The study followed the same group of families for 23 years, from 1984 to 2007, and discovered that the gap in wealth between white families and African-American families more than quadrupled during that period, from $20,000 to $95,000. Looking at financial assets excluding home equity, the study found that the median value of wealth held by white families increased from $22,000 to $100,000 during the period, while black families saw very little increase and had a median wealth of $5,000 in 2007.[46]

For the study to make sense you have to believe that race is the sole determinant of income. You have to believe that black people are condemned to live their lives in poverty and squalor. You have to ignore all of the wealthy and prosperous black people you see in the media and business. You definitely have to ignore the fact that between 1983 and 2001, the number of black households with net worth of $1 million or more increased 79 percent, from 61,000 households to 109,000.[47] These Black millionaires built their fortunes in large measure by owning their own businesses such as real estate, funeral homes, medical practices, construction, retail and service sector businesses. In short you have to

55

believe that the over 100,000 Black millionaires are exceptions to the rule and rest of us the black people are perpetual wards of the state.

The wealth gap studies only look at the dollars. They don't consider behavior or other societal factors. For instance, the cost of living in Manhattan, New York is much more expensive than the cost of living in Manhattan, Kansas. Should a teacher with 3 years experience in both of these places expect to make the same amount of money? The liberal media narrative dictates that you should fill studies with heartstring pulling sob stories while sprinkling in charts here and there. This particular story followed the same group of families for 23 years from 1984 to 2007. It only talks about their incomes and assets. The story didn't mention anything about their cost of living or behavior (which includes spending habits, frugality, location, or family composition.)

According to Jeff Humphreys, director of the Selig Center and the report's author, reported in August that U.S. Black buying power will total $845 billion in 2007 and is projected to top $1.1 trillion by 2012.[48] This is a perfect illustration proving that black people are not the helpless lot of human debris that the Liberals in the media and in government position us as. We are a financial juggernaut that has not realized its power. I know that through experience and studies like the one conducted by Mr. Humphreys, black people are not accumulating wealth because of lack of money, we are not accumulating wealth because of behavior. I have several relatives that have possessed thousands of dollars because of their hard work, and inheritance, and other ways, yet have little to show for it. Poor spending and investment habits are not exclusive to any group of Americans.

Ideas to counter it: You have to inform people that even the most "impoverished" Americans have a better standard of living than most people in the world. We have achieved this standard of living through hard work, innovation and the belief that we can profit from our sacrifice. As a result, wealth is created, and the fruits of the successful are shared among others. Our standard of living was not created by the government confiscating resources from producers and giving them to those that have no desire or ability to produce. Our standard of living has been created by inspiring the achievers and not pandering to those that willingly accept mediocrity or worse.

The best thing about America is that we have choices (at least we used to.) We are not condemned to the situations of our birth. Liberals want to convince the electorate that minorities are born in poverty and have no choice but to say there because of the "system." Their narrative dictates that people have no choice over their behavior.

From my experience as a 34 year old black man, I can tell you that a lot of black families like to spend money on things that make them feel good. When you look at black celebrities and blacks in the public, you will see a very opulent lifestyle. Go to any flea market in urban America and you will see many black people, spending their last dollar on the latest fashion, getting their hair and nails done, and making sure they have the best car they can afford. Is this behavior wrong? I don't think so. I believe that people are free to spend as they please with the understanding that all choices have consequences. However the studies are designed to make black people look like perpetual victims of unfairness so that liberals can use this information in order to transform the government into their socialist/communist desires. My relatives, like millions of other Americans, have collectively possessed and spent millions of dollars, with little to show for it. I can say with assurance that my people will never give up riding 1986 Cutlass Supremes sitting on 32 inch chrome wheels with candy paint, regardless of how short-lived, for the monotony of communism.

You have to convince people to believe that their individuality and God-given ability is sacred and unique. We all are different and it's senseless to compare ourselves to others. We all start at different places under different circumstances. Someone born into a wealthy family could squander all of his opportunity because of poor judgment. On the other hand, someone born in the worst situations could become very successful because of intestinal fortitude and seizing the opportunities given. When you accept the class warfare argument you willingly forfeit your individuality and decision making ability. Rugged individuality and the belief that you can conquer all adversity is what makes Americans different from others. When you have the belief that you can thrive in our country then the pittance that liberals offer will never be worth trading in the opportunity to excel.

Topic: Tolerance

Liberal Narrative: Liberals are tolerant, conservatives are intolerant

Barry White was known for many hits throughout the years. Although most of his hits were during the 1970s he had a comeback hit song in the 90s called *Practice What You Preach,* which I liked. Apparently, liberals have never heard the song because they believe that they are entitled to make the rules for everyone while they are exempted from them. Liberals and their friends in the media maintain the lie that liberals are tolerant. This lie is perpetuated primarily because of the imagery that they like to associate themselves with: images of Woodstock, flower power, peace signs, coexist bumper stickers and all of the fluff which they want you to associate them. In reality they are the complete opposite. When you study the history of tactics of liberalism, you realize that these images are another form of propaganda.

The truth is, liberals spend millions of dollars and countless hours of manpower in order to intimidate people, silence them and force them to follow their direction. Groups like "Media Matters", are well-financed machines used to monitor free speech in order to take snippets and use them to destroy people's careers. They do believe in free speech, but only for liberals. They behave as though that they are the arbiters of free speech. Talk show host Glenn Beck is one of their favorite targets.

If you listen to the propaganda from Media Matters you would never know that Glenn Beck is exercising the same constitutional rights that they enjoy. Liberals like to accuse others of "hate speech" during their profanity filled rants. Having been unsuccessful in their mission to remove Glenn Beck from the air, they have upped the ante in order to silence him. Media Matters announced that billionaire leftist George Soros donated $1 million in what Beck called a "bounty." Soros stated that the funds will be used "in an effort to more widely publicize the challenge Fox News poses to civil and informed discourse in our democracy."[49] I watch Fox News and listen to conservative radio shows because they speak from their position and support it with facts and citations. On the other hand, the left always accuses them of "hate speech" and "misinformation." They constantly attack the messenger and never the message. These elementary school tactics are recognized by rational adults and has led to America starting to realize that liberals are not the people they claim to be.

Here are just a few other stories that illustrate their "tolerance". Do a web search for the stories to see liberal "tolerance" in action:

- Protesters at 'Anti-hate' rally called Breitbart homosexual, spit on him[50]
- 5 charged in GOP tire slashings[51]

- Activist Group Puts Bounty on Head of Chamber of Commerce CEO[52]
- Blog Wants Celebs to Help Oust Lieberman's Wife From Susan Komen Ambassadorship[53]
- Obama: 'We Bring a Gun'[54]
- Protest Cancels Coulter Speech in Ottawa[55]
- Rock the Vote Asks Supporters to Withhold Sex to Pass Health Care Reform[56]

Ideas to counter it: The left wins when they are on the offense. You can expect them to fill the conversation with a lot of accusations and name-calling. This will keep you constantly defending your self and other conservatives. At the same time they are presented to be without flaw because they are constantly identifying yours. You need to come equipped with a laundry list of news stories and anecdotes of true liberalism in action. Force them agree to a uniform standard of misconduct and then start to slam them with your citations.

Topic: Racism

Liberal Narrative: Liberals are not racists, conservatives are racist

Liberals tend to get the biggest pass on racism because of the widely accepted undefined definition and imagery of a racist. The media and liberals have made it where conservatism and racism are synonymous. They want you to think that racist imagery include the Confederate flag, white Southern men, trucks with gun racks in the window, and even the American flag at times. Now that the left and the media has convinced much of the population that anything contrary to liberal positions is racist, they inject racism in every debate in order to have their way.

Former Democratic National Committee Chair Howard Dean, one of America's biggest racists, is no stranger to playing the race card instead of debating in the arena of ideas. What makes him a racist is not only his frequent use of the tactic, but the callous manner in which he exploits the most sensitive topic among African-Americans. Dean called the Tea Party movement "the last gasp of the generation that has trouble with diversity." He argued that, "The demographic changes we have all known were going to happen have happened and all of a sudden it is here for them and they don't know what to do.... Every morning when they see the president, they are reminded that things are totally different than they were when they were born."[57] He doesn't exploit racism out of concern for the plight of black Americans. He does it to undermine the political discussion in order to associate any opposition to liberalism with racism. Dean is reportedly worth more that $4million dollars.[58] I wonder how many black children benefit directly from his personal fortune? I wonder how many inner-city youth would he let in his home? If he is as benevolent with his wealth like most liberals, the answer is none. Liberals know that racism is their go-to tactic to put conservatives on the defense, and the mainstream media are willing accomplices. It's like repeatedly watching the same rerun of a sitcom. The jokes are no longer a surprise because you already know what's going to happen.

The Democratic Party and the media depend on Americans being ignorant and not to have an understanding of conservatism versus liberalism. They like to label conservatives as "extreme." This is a lie. The basics of both philosophies can be summarized like this:

Conservatism- *Belief in personal responsibility, limited government, free markets, individual liberty, traditional American values and a strong national defense. Believe the role of government should be to provide people the freedom necessary to pursue their own* goals. *Conservative policies generally emphasize empowerment of the individual to solve problems.*[59]

Liberalism- *The belief that governmental action is needed to achieve equal opportunity and equality for all, and that it is the duty of the State to alleviate social ills and to protect civil liberties and individual and human rights. Believe the role of the government should be to guarantee that no one is in need. Liberal policies generally emphasize the need for the government to solve people's problems.*[60]

Racism- *A belief or doctrine that inherent differences among the various human races determine cultural or individual achievement, usually involving the idea that one's own race is superior and has the right to rule others.*[61]

When you have an understanding of each philosophy you will find that by nature conservatives are not racists at all, in fact, they are indifferent to color because they believe each person has the ability to achieve greatness. On the other hand, the definitions of liberalism and racism are remarkably similar.

The government is run by people. People have biases. People have to decide who is "in need" and who is not. People decide when problems are problems and when problems are unbearable. People have to decide what is fair and what is unfair. These decisions have to be stripped from the individual. It's impossible for these people that run the government to not consider race and other factors when being the arbiters of fairness. It's liberals, not conservatives, who feel that they have to commandeer power in the form of the government in order to create some type of societal equilibrium based on their personal beliefs. Most Liberals are innately racist because they have decided that black people are condemned to be the perpetual underclass that cannot survive without their protection and intervention.

Ideas to counter it: If you are a conservative being accused of being a racist, this is when you need to have faith in your beliefs. Here are three steps that will help you not only defend your position but put the blame where it belongs at the feet of liberals.

1) **Understand the race game**. They need to realize that no matter what they do or say, the Democratic Party and the liberals in the media are going to accuse them of being racists. Therefore, they need to have a firm understanding of what they believe, and stand by it, because by nature conservatives are not racists. Never accept any of their premises because they are designed to keep you on the defense. State that you are not a racist and be done with it. Do not dwell in this conversation; the longer you stay in the conversation, the more likely you will say something you regret. Your opposition's comments are designed to make you say something "dumb" so that they can continue to pounce on it. Insist that you do not believe someone's color dictates their way of thinking, their aptitude or their ability to succeed. You believe that every American has an opportunity to succeed without the intervention of government deciding their fate. Then move on!

Remember that the mere acceptance of conservative beliefs is the equivalent of racism to most liberals. It is unlikely that you will convince them otherwise. Therefore it is in your best interest to understand their objective and not be a victim in their stupid game.

2) **Articulate conservatism**. Be able to explain the difference between conservatism, liberalism, and racism. Explain why liberalism and racism are virtually the same whereas conservatism is the opposite. If you truly

believe in the conventional conservative philosophy, then you are indifferent to someone's color because you innately believe that their character will decide their fate. Conservatives need to articulate that liberals are innately racist because they have given themselves the power to decide what's best for certain groups of people that they intentionally categorize as being "disenfranchised." For example, liberals don't consider black people as equals. If they did they would insist that black people (and everyone else) be free to make their own decisions and deal with the consequences of them.

3) **Insist on discussing serious issues**. Liberals will want to stay engaged in emotionally charged rhetorical arguments because this is where they have the advantage. Conservatives are most effective when they articulate common sense solutions that people can identify with. Insist on offering solutions to serious issues like the federal deficit, out-of-control spending, and immigration. Let the liberals continue to dwell in racism because that is where they are comfortable. When they continue to dwell, ask them why they continue to dwell on race when there are so many more important issues at hand.

Topic: Taxes
Liberal Narrative: Conservatives only care about the rich and hate the middle-class and poor
Many fail to realize that the issue of taxes is not only about economics, but it is also a moral issue. Liberals want to frame the argument that conservatives don't want to pay any taxes and that is not true. Conservatives understand taxes have to be paid in order to run the government. We understand that the military has to be funded, roads have to be preserved, bridges have to be built and police are needed to maintain order in the streets. The issue is not only how these resources are spent, but how much is enough to take from one individual in order

to not only fund the government but to fund other citizens (and non-citizens through foreign aid for example) and special interests. Many call it the redistribution of wealth.

Income redistribution in its crudest form is taking resources from producers and giving them to consumers. While many will agree that our government should have some type of assistance to those that have fallen on hard times, the issue becomes how much should they be given and at what cost to society? Liberals will argue that the more you make then the more you should pay. This logic has led to combined tax rates of over 50% in many states for top earners. The question becomes, will an individual be productive knowing that half of his earnings will be confiscated by the government and that someone that is capable of producing will have a share of his earnings because they choose not to produce? Do high tax rates provide incentive to produce wealth or scale back your productivity?

Liberals believe that they are entitled to spend the people's money better than that they can. They also feel entitled to the earnings of others in order to pay for their benevolence. Liberals love to "tax the rich" because they believe that some people (not wealthy liberals like the Kennedys and George Soros) reach a point where they have enough money. Since this person has excessive funds, the government should take the fruits of their labor and give it to others that really need it. The politician will then appropriate the funding, let's say for a new swimming pool, take credit for building the pool and then name it after himself as though he purchased the pool with his own funds. Instead of the producer deciding to use the fruits of his labor to fund causes that he believes in, the government spends his money on endless bureaucracy to fund their alleged benevolence.

65

Ideas to counter it:

This is when you have to press them to reveal numbers and explain the practical application of their ideas. They will want go around in circles stating that the tax code should be fair and that the ones that benefit the most from the system should pay there "fair share." Ask them how much that is. Tell them to define numerically how much is rich, middle-class and poor. Ask them how much someone should pay in taxes in order to be spared from the liberals' constant barrage of guilt trips. Should an individual and/or a family making more than $250,000 a year pay 50%, 60% or 70% of their income to the government? Should the government confiscate all of their earnings at some point? Make them explain how increasing someone's tax burden will make them more productive. Make them explain how increasing taxes on products will encourage people to purchase more. Don't we all benefit from roads and bridges? What about the shared sacrifice liberals lecture us about? Should some people be exempted from this mandate?

The likelihood of them giving a number is small. Their goal is to perpetuate the feel-good rhetoric in order to mask their intent of using the tax code to conduct social engineering. You want them to reveal their true intent, and that is the last thing they want to do. They thrive on ambiguity and innuendo. Your beliefs on taxes can be defended and it is not about making one group pay more than another. It is about lowering rates for everyone so that they choose to be as productive or unproductive as they please, as well as limiting the size and scope of government. Conservatives and Liberals understand that the more government gets, the more it spends. One group says that the people should spend their own money and the other group says the government will spend it better.

5

Creating Your Voice

Technology has lowered the barriers of entry to almost every field of endeavor especially the media. All it takes is a few minutes to set up your own blog, website, or Internet radio show. It doesn't matter if you have talent or no talent, great material or lousy material, all you need is access to a computer. Technology has allowed anyone the ability to reach millions of people virtually for free. It's no surprise that this accessibility makes way for millions of carbon copies. So how does one cut through the clutter?

In order to be successful in a time when so many people are competing for attention, you have to follow a rule that is not new at all. You have to create your own voice. You have to be distinct and authentic. Long before the Internet, people that were original and authentic were the ones that became successful and iconic. Conservatives revere Ronald Reagan because of his ability to communicate and his unwavering commitment to the principles that he believed in. Many politicians will say anything and morph into any form in order to win elections but Reagan stayed true to his conservative beliefs. Elvis Presley, John Wayne, Shirley Chisholm, Michael Jackson, Madonna, Martin Luther King Jr. and so many other figures we hold dear will have lasting legacies because they created distinct brand equities.

The most successful people create trends rather than follow them. In order to do this you have to create what is called a brand equity. Brand equity simply means "what is your name worth?" or "What is the perceived value of your name?" If you can't answer this question no one else can. Even if you don't plan on being a media personality, it's still important for each of us to answer this question because it is beneficial to understand in our daily lives. We should be aware of how we view ourselves and how others view us. This is not to say you should conform to the world, in fact it is the opposite. It is a way of controlling how you are viewed by the world.

In politics, controlling one's brand equity is vital to success. Politicians spend a great deal of money and resources to build personas and then maintain them. They also work very hard to define their opponent's brand equity. If you haven't built a solid brand equity, it's very easy for your opponent to assign one to you. During elections we're used to seeing "attack ads." Attack ads are used to destroy the brand equity of an opponent. If the public doesn't understand what the politician stands for, they easily fall prey to the messages of attack ads. This is why politicians invest in building brand equity. What does this have to do with dealing with the media? Everything. The media is the vehicle used to create and destroy brand equity.

A savvy person that is prepared and equipped with the right tools can either use the media to magnify his message or be mitigated by it. There are several steps you need to take in order to prepare for any type of interaction with the media. However, before taking on the media you need to have a good idea of how you want to be portrayed and what is it that you want to conveyed. Let's first discuss creating our own brand equity. I like to call it your voice.

During my first attempt at public office, I was unsuccessful in securing a seat on Cincinnati's City Council in 2007. Cincinnati has a nine-member council comprised of all at-large seats. This is considered one of the most difficult and expensive councils to get elected to because of the size of the city (geographical and population). Although the race is nonpartisan, both parties (in addition to a local third-party called the Charterites) endorse candidates. While Southwest Ohio is known as one of the most conservative regions in the country, the city of Cincinnati is predominately Democrat. In 2007, all nine incumbents were running for re-election. Of the field of 25 candidates roughly 19 had either sat on or had previously run for City Council. To further magnify adversity, on a slate of seven Republican candidates, I was arguably the most philosophically conservative so my biggest challenge was presenting myself to the community in a way they would embrace, while staying true to my beliefs. Instead of trying to conform to conventional campaign wisdom, I decided to focus on my image and beliefs with the volume turned way up.

My campaign staff and I decided that we were going to win or lose as Andre Harper. I selectively chose which interviews I would take. I wore a beard instead of being clean-shaven. I didn't always wear a suit. I would wear a polo, slacks and loafers to make public events. I wanted people to know that I was young, intelligent, and willing to show both my bravado and my credentials.

My candidacy presented many other challenges. At 29 years old, I was the youngest candidate. I was a staunch conservative in a largely Democrat city. I am a proud graduate of a historically black college whose philosophical heroes include Booker T. Washington, Malcolm X., Marcus Garvey, the Honorable Elijah Muhammad, Ronald Reagan and Barry Goldwater. When I went to black neighborhoods, I was naturally dismissed because I was a Republican. I took my message of conservatism all over the city. Many white people didn't understand me because I was discussing how the city of Cincinnati will benefit from the teachings of Malcolm X. and Ronald Reagan in the same sentence. While I didn't win, I found my voice and a way to deliver my message with integrity and honesty. I not only gained the respect of my community, but I was able to look in the mirror and respect the person I saw. I realized that I could create a successful public persona by being myself. You, too, can do this to but you have to understand authenticity.

Authenticity constantly requires reinforcement, and it can come from a number of sources: craftsmanship, timeliness, relevance. It is your brand's values, the emotional connection it makes, that truly define its authenticity. There are four primary strands that draw out that connection.[62]

- **A sense of place.** "Authenticity comes from a place we can connect with," says Steve McCallion, creative director of Ziba, a Portland, Oregon--based design consultancy. "A place with a story."[63] Ronald Reagan frequently referred to America as "the shining city on a hill." While this is not a real place, people connected with the imagery because it spoke to a lot of things. It touched on his optimism, it created a goal, and people connected with his vision to create a country that they wanted to live in and leave to their children.

- **A strong point of view.** Authenticity also emerges from "people with a deep passion for what they are doing," says McCallion. [64] It doesn't matter if you love or hate Rush

Limbaugh, you know where he stands. You know what you're going to get from Rush, and that's pure conservatism. In a world with so many conservative voices, Rush stands out above the rest, not just because he was the original, but because of his distinct ability to articulate his positions clearly while being entertaining.

- **Serving a larger purpose.** People aren't stupid. They know that when they see you on TV or listen to you on the radio, they know that you're either trying to sell them a product or persuade their thinking. But if a brand can convincingly argue that its position has a larger purpose, authenticity sets in. "Just as there are purpose-driven lives," says Character's Hardison, "there are purpose-driven brands."[65] The Tea Party movement is successful primarily because it connected with people's desire to stop massive growth of our government. The moderate voters that voted Republican in 2010 were probably persuaded to vote alongside the Tea Party not because they are all conservatives, but because they connect with the idea that our government was getting out of hand with its growth and spending. Regardless if you are conservative, moderate or liberal, everyone will pay the price if the government continues to grow at the pace it's going.

- **Integrity.** Authenticity comes to a brand that is what it says it is. In other words, "the story that the brand tells through its actions aligns with the story it tells through its communications," Hardison says. "Only then will customers sense that the brand's story is true."[66] It's no secret that registered Democrats outnumber registered Republicans in most states. Yet Republicans continue to win elections across the country despite registration disadvantages and a one-sided media. Why? Republicans win when they are true to their values and able to articulate them. Conservatism resonates with

71

American values, so people can identify with Republican candidates. People understand that you can't spend more money than you earn. People understand that if you don't work, you don't eat. People understand the importance of personal responsibility instead of depending on someone else to feed you. "In fact, while all 50 states are, to some degree, more conservative than liberal (with the conservative advantage ranging from 1 to 34 points), Gallup's 2009 party ID results indicate that Democrats have significant party ID advantages in 30 states and Republicans in only 4," said an analysis of the survey results published by Gallup. "Despite the Democratic Party's political strength seen in its majority representation in Congress and in state houses across the country more Americans consider themselves conservative than liberal," said Gallup's analysis.[67]

One should never take the media lightly, especially if they know that you are politically conservative. It doesn't matter if you're at a county fair or standing on the floor of the political convention, what you say (and possibly how you look) could be broadcast to millions of people in a matter of seconds. You don't know who is listening, it could be someone that is in dire need of what you are offering or someone that was once a supporter and is now embarrassed because of your portrayal. This is why it is important to have control of your image. You want to make sure that you're always prepared to communicate your position in the way that you desire.

Everyone knows the old adage, "if you fail to plan, you plan to fail." This statement should be chiseled into your brain. If you decide to take part in any type of political engagement or movement, especially a conservative one like the Tea Party, you'd better be ready to deal with the media at any time. Since the inception of the Tea Party in 2009, I have watched many Tea Party activists interviewed at rallies that were simply voicing their concerns. The sound bites were then repackaged in a newsroom in order to purposely miscommunicate the entire meaning of the movement. If you're going to attend Tea Parties, you need to be able to have your impromptu interview game plan together.

An impromptu interview is when a reporter is at an event and looks around for someone to interview. These interviews typically last less than five minutes of which only seconds will be used in the broadcast. Only the most newsworthy statement from the subject will be used. Understanding this, it is important to make sure that everything you say is able to be put into the context that you want it in. For instance take this fictional example of an interview that took place at a Tea Party event in 2010.

Situation

Reporter: Hello Joe, why are you here at the Tea Party?
Joe: I am here because I am tired of what's happening in our country. It's time for us to take our country back because we don't like what Obama is doing. He and the rest of his people are turning our country into a socialist nation.

Evening Newscast

Reporter: This is Barbara Jackson reporting from the Tea Party rally downtown. Many of these people are very upset with the president and have decided to take action.
Joe's comment: It's time for us to take our country back because we don't like what Pres. Obama is doing.

Reporter: He is not alone there a couple hundred people gathered shouting and holding up signs with unflattering pictures of the president.

If you were a casual viewer of the news and you saw the story packaged in this way you probably would have a negative image of the Tea Party movement. You will probably start to believe that they are simply a violent group of Obama haters instead of a segment of society that disagree with his policies. While Joe's objection may be based purely on his philosophical disagreements with the president, his words could be used against him by the mainstream media. No one expects Joe to be a media guru but there are few things Joe and people like Joe could learn in order to better improve how they and their causes are portrayed in the media.

Savvy journalists can take statements out of context by simply isolating them. Long sentences are easily taken out of context when you don't purposely put context around them.

For instance, I was preparing a speech for a Tea Party rally in New Orleans, and I wanted to discuss how Democrats believe they own black people's votes. At first I was going to say:

As a African-American, self identified conservative, many Democrats use racist names like Uncle Tom to describe me because I don't agree with them. For some reason, they feel entitled to my vote. Democrats should pass a law stating that all Black people born in the United States should be Democrat. That way we don't have to endure their racism.

After reviewing the statements and reading the speech aloud, I realized that this could be taken out of context in many ways particularly the line

74

Democrats should pass a law stating that all Black people born in the United States should be Democrat. In an interview I'd be forced to play defense and that's where they want you. So I had to change the speech in order to get my point across but also add context within the potentially controversial statements.

Since Democrats expect blacks to support them, I challenge you to pass a law stating every black baby born in the United States will be committing treason if they fail to support the Democratic Party

The point of adding context to your statements is to make sure that when media begins to fragment them, it will be difficult for them to use a statement because it doesn't make sense unless it's accompanied with the rest of the sentence. They would either have to include your thought fully or risk using such a small bite that makes no sense to the viewer. They have done this before as well, but people can recognize it.

Interview Preparation

Have a clear message that you want the audience to receive
Don't have more than a three-pronged message. Most people will only take away three things from a message. Keep it simple and effective instead of long and complex. If the message is concise, it is much easier for them to remember your message.

Decide if this interview will give you the opportunity to make your point and provide helpful information about your topic/issue/organization.
All interviews are not good interviews. I have learned that it is not good to accept every interview opportunity. You have to make sure that you are going to be given the opportunity to present your side. When I was

promoting my first book, **Political Emancipation**, I had the misfortune of doing an interview on a syndicated radio show with a national audience. I didn't do my preparation, and didn't realize that this was a shock jock show that used someone who acted as an antagonist (more like a clown) as the co-host. Instead of me talking about my book, I spent two segments playing the dozens with the antagonist. It was totally not worth it. Had I done my research I would have found that although this person has over 1 million listeners, this wasn't the reading demographic and the show itself is about entertainment and not serious discussion about the issues. Some shows bring guests on for the sole purpose of embarrassing them. If a Republican decides to accept an interview from the *Daily Show with Jon Stewart*, he'd better be ready for anything. It is important to be selective with interviews because one bad interview could go viral and ruin everything you have worked so hard to build. Remember, the host has a continual platform to explain his views, but you only have a few minutes, or seconds.

Know your message tracks

Write down and practice message tracks in brief statements or bullet points. Be able to memorize them. It's best to have them bulleted so that they are easy to remember and repeat. If you are part of a group, make sure everyone has the same message! If you are meeting with more than one media outlet, make sure your messages are consistent with each reporter.

Speak clearly and concisely

Remove jargon or long explanations. Most people aren't experts on the topics like you are. You have to speak in a manner and vocabulary that most people can comprehend. Avoid acronyms and long soliloquies. An effective communicator is able to "humanize" himself or organization. For example: "Don't talk about saving 30,000 barrels of oil. Talk in terms of an extra three tanks of gasoline for the car of every viewer or listener."[68]

Be ready to cite sources and gives statistics when asked

Don't volunteer any information outside of your primary message. Don't give out any information that you can't support. Be ready to give citations and /or statistics to support your points when appropriate. Review facts and figure before the interview so you are comfortable discussing them.

Anticipate questions and be ready to respond appropriately

Whenever you accept an interview, you should have a good idea about what is going to be discussed. For instance, if you are a Tea Party activist that has been invited to an interview, the likelihood is that the interviewer will want to discuss your role in the movement, what you believe, and what activities you have planned. It's highly unlikely that the entire interview will center around the NFL playoffs. With this knowledge of subject, it becomes easier to prepare and anticipate what you will be asked. Prepare a list of tough and timely questions and then answer them. Practice with a colleague or in front of the mirror. This feels uncomfortable at first but it's worth it. I can guarantee you, it's much more uncomfortable to be in an interview that you are not prepared for.

Understand the media outlet

You need to understand the media outlet that you are being interview by, and what type of program is. It is also very important to know the target audience. The target audience are the people that watch/listen to the program. To be an effective communicator you have to cater your message to the audience. This is different from pandering. Pandering is telling people what they want to hear. You can cater your message and still be true to your beliefs. For instance, if you are a politician running for office and you are being interview by Oprah Winfrey, you need to be prepared to discuss why women's issues are so important and what you are doing to address them. When you are being interview by Sean Hannity, you need to be prepared to discuss your conservative values and how they guide your decision-making process. Connecting with your audience is the best way to score a winning interview.

Know interview format

It may not seem that important, but the interview format is very important to know and plan for. You need to know the interview format, length, whether it is live or taped, solo or multi-guests. Taped interviews can be particularly dangerous because they can be edited and re-packaged. You have no control of this. So it is important that you are able to talk in sound bites.

Taped Interviews- Talking in Sound Bites

- Keep your message short and simple- 10 seconds
- Sometimes you have to keep repeating your message because the interviewer may be looking to use your words against you. Remember that they will edit it. Edit yourself, don't let them edit you
- Put pauses in your answers, think about what you're saying, don't just say what comes to mind
- Stay on message because people are always willing to take your answers out of context
- Present your message and then stop. Don't try to fill that space. Diarrhea of the mouth is a recipe for disaster.

Opposition research

"Keep your friends close and your enemies closer" is a good rule of thumb when dealing with politics. You need to do research on the opposition group or person. Understand their beliefs and objectives. Know their history to the best of your ability and have an idea of the basis of your disagreement. When preparing for an interview, ask as many questions from the producer beforehand as possible. You could expect that they are doing their homework so don't take the risk of being unprepared because the audience will contrast both sides. First impressions are lasting and hard to reestablish.

Don't give them ammunition

If you are conservative, the media is always looking to take your statements and run with them. On the other hand, when liberals make gaffes they close ranks and bury them immediately. Your statements will be circulated in the media echo chamber until they have destroyed you. They are always looking for mistakes. To combat this you have to speak concisely. Your words should be used like an entrée not a buffet. Once you serve them your answer, stop. They will try to press you because they want you to say something that you didn't intend to say. Keep repeating your answer until they move on. Savvy journalists can keep asking you the same question a different way. They do this when they are searching for a specific answer. Don't fall for the bait.

Important Questions to ask yourself before an interview

- Can the media take any of my statements out of context?
- What does the audience already know? (Background)
- What do I want the audience to remember?
- Are there examples of pictures I can paint for them?
- What action do I want the audience to take?

79

Message Development

In order to be an effective communicator you need to be able to develop clear message objectives. Identify your communication objectives. Decide in advance what you want the audience to take away from your appearance. "One of the tools I use with corporate leaders is 'OSTA': objective, strategy, tactics, and audience," says Mike Paul of MGP & Associates in New York. "Everything communicated should have an OSTA plan of attack. "Plan to hammer home your key messages. For interviews, keep answers - especially for TV or radio - to about 25 to 40 seconds each. When it's appropriate, use props or visual materials to vary your pacing.[69] Here are some basic concerns when preparing effective messages:

- What is my main message?
- Use short, clear sentences
- Use seventh grade level grammar
- Use statistics and examples to support/bolster the premise

The following is an example of an effective message:

POOR	*XYZ company is a good neighbor*
BETTER	*XYZ company is concerned about protecting the environment*
EFFECTIVE	*XYZ company voluntarily spent $5 million last year on a program to clean the Hudson River, making us a good neighbor concerned about protecting the environment.*[70]

Research

- Who is the audience? Know details about the show (religious or secular, conservative or liberal, men or women, etc.)
- Know about the host
- Know the issues important the audience and speak to them
- Is the host is a traditional journalist or opinion driven?

- Is doing the show is worth it?
- Will the questions be heard by the audience? Some producers just use the answers in a news package

Dealing with the media can be a daunting task. However, being prepared and realistic will position you to get your message out in the way that you want it portrayed, regardless of the media outlet.

6

Dealing With the Media

It doesn't matter if you are a conservative purposely seeking to provide commentary or a passionate patriot attending a Tea Party rally that suddenly finds a camera in his face, you need to understand that the mainstream media is not your friend. It has never been your friend and hell could freeze over before it becomes your friend. While they may pretend to be your friend, you should never be lured into a false sense of security or you will pay the price. Conservatives that are willing to sacrifice their values in order to become a token find themselves losing the respect of the people that they claim to share ideology with in order to win favor with people that will never accept their differences.

Conservatives need to have a "come-to-Jesus moment" before engaging the mainstream media. Most conservatives that I have met tend to be realists. We see the world as it is and not how we would like it to be. When dealing with the media you have to take the same approach. You have to accept that in matters of politics, our contemporary mainstream media has drawn a line in the sand and chose a side to stand on. It just so happens that we are not on the same side. It is becoming increasingly evident that there are not only double standards for conservatives and liberals in the media, the mainstream media has elected to use all of its might to discredit conservatives while advancing liberal ideology at all costs.

Conservatives like Sarah Palin understand that the game is fixed. She is under constant assault from every direction for being herself. The way she is treated is an abomination to decency. Liberals give more sympathy to convicted rapists, murders and child molesters than to law-abiding citizens that don't accept their socialist worldview. After another routine sexual slur from the racist Bill Maher, and no support from so-called feminist organizations, Palin shrugged it off saying, "I'm through whining about a liberal press that holds particularly conservative women to a different standard, because it doesn't do any good to whine about it." She continued, "Nobody ever promised life was going to be fair."[71]

I don't say this to scare you but it is what it is. Instead of acting like a liberal by complaining how unfair life is, you have to create strategies to deal with obstacles you will encounter. It is almost inevitable that you're going to deal with interviewers that don't share your point of view. The founders of our nation envisioned a free press where the personal political views of the interviewer would not matter. Their job was to be objective and to seek the facts in order to inform the public. Unfortunately, that has changed. As a conservative, you're not only going to deal with media personalities that disagree with you, but it will seem as though they have a sworn duty to discredit your position as well as take it a step further by trying to assassinate your character and destroy your livelihood for the sake of perpetuating liberal narratives.

This chapter is designed to primarily help you prepare to deal with supposedly unbiased interviewers that clearly have conflicting views. Liberal intimidation groups like Media Matters masquerade under the guise of protecting the integrity of journalism, but like to attack Fox

News and talk radio by making the claim that they are biased. The truth is that the elitists that seek to limit First Amendment rights for political adversaries don't want you to understand the difference between news and opinion journalism. The concept of opinion journalism should be simple enough so even the people at Media Matters understand. They are not intended to be unbiased like the people at the news desk. The problem is not with opinion shows like Rush Limbaugh, Sean Hannity, and Chris Matthews, the problem is when news anchors and reporters inject their blatant biases into what is supposed to be reporting facts.

The media is the beast that you will have to face. You should not be intimidated by this. They serve a purpose. They are providing the opportunity to give your message to a large audience. So this is something you should be happy about! However, from their perspective they are using this as an opportunity to advance their narrative. Remember that political interviews are like sporting events. They are a test of will. Both players are trying to impose their will on the other. You need to have this mindset going into every interview.

In my opinion, Ronald Reagan is the best example of a conservative that used the media to his advantage. I am sure that President Reagan knew that the media was not in his corner, however he was able to win two landslide presidential victories without the help of conservative talk radio or the Internet. How did he do it? He did it through effective communication. He had a game plan and he stuck to it.

A part of his early campaign strategy was to emphasize the importance of effective communication and how leaders throughout history were remembered for the things they said more so than the things that they did. Communication was indeed one of his strengths so it was important that he emphasize it throughout his campaigns.

He also was able to speak through the reporter. What do I mean by this? Reagan, as well as President Clinton, were masters of deploying his message tracks. When the reporter asked the question, he made sure that he replied with the information that he wanted the viewer's to comprehend. This means that sometimes you'll answer the question asked and sometimes you won't. A skilled interviewee is at peace with this tactic.

Remember the purpose of doing an interview is to get your point across, not to become a punching bag for the host. You take the reporter's question and use it as a vehicle to get your point across. You can do this in many ways. You have to always get back to your message. You have to stay on message. Here are three examples:

The Good

On January 10, 1991, Larry King interviewed Ronald Reagan American about the situation in Iraq.

REAGAN: ... I think that one of the things, one of the arguments that's going on in our country with the Congress is helping Saddam Hussein. And that is that our Congress -- and I hope within the next 48 hours all this will be done -- our Congress should pass a resolution that they will be behind the president if he has to take military action or not.

KING: Do you agree, Mr. President, that they should debate it?

REAGAN: Well, but I do -- if that's what it's going to take to get a vote from them. But what we need is to get rid of a situation that is now, I think, strengthening the stubbornness of Saddam Hussein. When he sees our government supposedly divided here between the Congress and the president, now if the Congress says yes, commander in chief, and so forth, and if he takes this action, we will be supportive of him.

KING: What do you do, though, with this dilemma? And you've been someone all your life who has spoken out on issues. Ronald Reagan, when you were a Democrat you spoke out, when you were a Republican, you were president, whether you were in the senate -- whether you were, rather, governor of California, an actor, you spoke out. Shouldn't you, if you sit in the Senate tonight and you don't favor this, shouldn't you say so? Or are you saying no?

REAGAN: Well, I suppose that they have to argue and debate, but I would have to say to anyone who is sitting in that body and is disagreeing with regard to what must be done, if necessary, to change this situation, I'd do my best to persuade them they were on the wrong side.

KING: Do you think they should not stand up? In other words, do you think they should disagree in private?

REAGAN: Well, they might disagree in private, but I think they -- I think that our government has to recognize always, and sometimes I don't think it does, it has to recognize that we, the people, are in charge of this system in this country. We're unlike almost any nation on earth, and the representatives and the government employees and officeholders work for the people. The employer is out there, the American people. And I think they should keep that in mind. [72]

King was trying to get Reagan to take a position on whether or not the United States should invade Iraq. He used Reagan's position as a former president as a basis to make this observation. He answered with his classic optimism and belief in our system and at the same time put the onus on the sitting members of Congress and the president.

The Bad

Rep. Sheila Jackson-Lee was interviewed by Fox News host Greta Van Susteren to discuss the healthcare debate of 2009. Citizens filled town hall meetings hosted by congressional leaders in order to make their voices heard about the issue. Rep. Jackson-Lee came under fire because she was caught on camera talking on a cell phone while one of her constituents was trying to ask her a question. It appeared as though she was completely ignoring the constituent. She argued that she was calling a hotline to get an answer because apparently she didn't have a clue about how the healthcare bill worked, that she vehemently supported and voted for.[73]

During the interview, Jackson-Lee seemed to do her best to portray the negative image of a self-absorbed diva instead of a public servant. Instead of conducting a respectful conversation, she was rude. She spent nearly the entire interview talking over Van Susteren, repeating the same messages over and over, and blatantly not addressing any of the concerns of the host. Even in the rare moments Jackson-Lee was silent, she would then interrupt Van Susteren by saying "go ahead I'm listening." "Here's the problem... Let me explain something to you... One of the problems is you're not listening, and that was sort of the criticism that you weren't listening, you're on the phone..." Van Susteren said out of frustration. While Jackson-Lee's tactics may be interpreted as rude, she was effective in the sense that she stuck to her game plan and message track. I am sure that she accepted the interview with the assumption that there will be little agreement with the host and her audience. Therefore, she went all-out and spoke over the host and talked loudly over the course of the interview so she could just get it over with.

The Ugly

Upstart senatorial candidate Alvin Greene shocked the world when he became the Democratic Senate nominee in South Carolina in 2010. On an interview on MSNBC, the most politically safe venue for a Democrat, Alvin Greene showed just how much he was out of his league. If you ignore the fact that Greene came off as totally unprepared, you'll realize that he did do a few things right. Please understand that I am not advocating that someone perform like Greene did during this interview. I am saying that there is a lot to learn from Greene's misfortune. His goal was to make sure that anyone that watched that interview went away knowing that DeMint started the recession. Even when the host asked Greene about the origins of his nick name, he used transitions and replied with "DeMint started the recession." In a very crude manner, Greene did what an effective communicators do. He stayed on message. The answer to every question was the same "DeMint started the recession."[74]

Message Delivery

While content is the meat of your presentation, the delivery is like the gravy, garnish and other accompaniments that enhance the attractiveness of the presentation. On the other hand, I am a believer in substance over style. I listen to what is said and not how things are said. I am not like most people. Most people care about how things are presented. You have to understand of this dynamic before you enter the public realm.

Verbal Delivery

An effective communicator is a person that not only is able to be concise, but can use their words to create images in the minds of the listener. If a person can see what it is that you're saying, you stand a good chance of persuading them.

- Paint pictures so the audience can visualize your message
- Use examples they can relate to as much as possible
- Use statistics to support your position, keep it simple
- Use references and statistics from liberal sources as much as possible
- Always be able to cite your sources
- Use statistics that can connect with tangible examples people can relate to, for example, "this policy will increase the average families costs by $800 a year." Instead of saying "drilling in Alaska will result in X billions in barrels for the US," use "drilling in Alaska will result in 30 years of energy for the US."

Create Custom Phrases

When you are being interviewed you need to always steer the interview back to your message. The interviewer will do his best to control the interview and you have to have the same goal. It is a test of wills. However, your time is limited so you have more pressure to get your message out. One way to get your message out is to create custom taglines. Custom phrases are transitions that you can use to always come back to your message. If you are trying to sell your book about state government and the interviewer asks you a seemingly unrelated question asked you a question about the football playoffs, you want to initially address the question with a get back to your message track. You will say something like "football playoffs have a great deal of benefit to our society and this is another reason why it's important to maintain a healthy state government."

Examples

"and once again nothing is more important than health care"

"this is government once again taking more of our liberties away" "here is yet another example of the divisive class warfare rhetoric that continues the divide this country"

Transitions

Like custom phrases, transitions are used to steer the direction of the interview back in your favor. When being interviewed by a reporter or a debate with an adversary, their goal is to control the flow of the conversation. Your goal is the same. When you are asked questions that could be detrimental to your argument you have to steer away from them. Instead of answering them directly, you have to present your point of view that disputes the claim of your opponent. The way to do this is by using a transition.

Examples

"the real issue is..."

"The bottom line is..."

"Our audience cares about..."

Hillary Clinton mastered the art of transitioning. On a 60 Minutes interview, Hillary and then Governor Bill Clinton were faced with allegations that her husband was not faithful in their marriage. When continuously pressed concerning the allegations of her husband's affairs, she kept on transitioning to raise the point that there are more pressing issues to discuss and that their personal lives are private. She further answered that it should be the people who will decide when voting whether their refusal to discuss the allegations is appropriate. In essence, Hillary Clinton took control of the interview through the art of transitioning.[75]

Personal Appearance

Researchers have found that how you communicate - what you look like and how you sound - can be far more important than what you say when it comes to getting your message across. Research out of UCLA found that when what is communicated is out of alignment with how it is communicated, the nonverbal cues, such as tone of voice, eye movement, posture, hand gestures and facial expressions, overwhelm what is verbalized. Albert Mehrabian's study found that nonverbal communication accounted for 93 percent of a presenter's impact. The important point of the research is that it's essential that the nonverbal and verbal elements of a presentation be aligned.[76]

Body Language

"Even in positive interview situations, interviewees sometimes look tense or stiff, which can have a big impact on credibility," says Gail Gardner of Adamson Public Relations in St. Louis. Before on-camera interviews, if there is time, do some exercises or walk around to relax your body.[77]

- Use hand gestures on TV. They make you look comfortable.
- Don't use hand gestures to take away eye contact or to compete with your face.
- Nothing about hand gestures should be memorable
- Never shuffle papers
- Never point at people

Face

Facial expressions contribute to nonverbal communication and can have a significant impact on a spokesperson's ability to connect with the audience and get his or her point across. Researchers have found that people can identify with great accuracy seven separate human emotions, even after seeing only facial and eye expressions. These include sadness, happiness, anger, fear, surprise, disgust and interest. Beginning very early in life, typically before a child's first birthday, people begin building skills that enable them to accurately read the faces of people around them. As a result, without speaking a word, a facial expression can convey a great deal of information to others. People watch a speaker's face during a presentation or media interview. When you speak, your face -- more clearly than any other part of your body -- communicates to others your attitudes, feelings and emotions.[78]

- Dramatize facial expressions (exaggerate your expressions). Since TV is two-dimensional, you will have to magnify your expressions in order to look more natural
- Be energetic to capture attention (as well as provide entertainment value)
- Smile - Use a natural smile, not a fake cheesy grin
- Have a pleasant look when speaking
- Make eye contact. Look towards the person you are talking to and look at the interviewer during one-to-one or look at the camera doing satellite interviews
- Make sure you know which camera is on

Clothing
- Dress relative to the forum
- You are judged on how you look
- Blue and red's are best. Avoid white because it projects light
- Gray suits are better than black
- Blue or off-white shirts are best
- Be careful of patterns, don't wear anything distracting (no logos or pins, unless it's a US flag)
- Wear clothing they can attach a microphone to

Going on offense

An effective communicator uses every opportunity to go on the offense. This is all about control. This means that you want to constantly try to control the flow of the conversation and make sure that your point is being made to the audience. Politicians are known for offense during interviews. Political interviews are generally adversarial versus other interviews that seek to get information (i.e. an upcoming concert or Girl Scout cookie sales). There is a great deal of power that comes with being the subject of an interview. Politicians understand that they have the ability to shape the discussion based on his or her answers.

In order to stay on offense you have to continuously stay on message. When presented with questions that could lure you away from your key messages, use your transitions in order to bring the interview back in your direction. In the case of a debate with a counterpart, keep in mind that your adversary has the same mission and will probably be using similar tactics. Remember it's better to have a stalemate than be defeated. Use transitions and message tracks to keep the conversation under your control. This gets monotonous at times (and frustrating to viewers), but it is the key to effectively communicating your point of view.

Playing Defense

I would love to say that if you stay on message you will always be on offense. In reality you will find yourself on defense. There are tactics that you need to have in your repertoire when you find your back against the wall.

When Under Attack

- When you are attacked use heartwarming stories like "let me give you an example", followed by a story or statistic
- Try to use a tag line after each statement to reinforce your point

- Briefly address their concern and then transition into your talking point/message and then tagline
- Maintain your composure, keep your personality, polish who you are
- Don't repeat charges made against you. For example, if someone says "You want to eliminate the Department of Education!" respond with "I want to hold teachers to tougher standards."
- Always think about your word choice. Use phrases that will resonate with people. Use phrases that will hurt your opponent i.e. accusing them of "flip-flopping."
- Being able to smile during debates makes you appear more confident. You have to be able to have a positive demeanor while attacking your opponent. **You must always be likable**!

You don't have to answer every question

Sometimes a reporter asks you a question that you can't answer. This is a point when you have to be honest with yourself. You have several options here.

1) You can be honest and say that you don't know and that you will get back to them with an answer. This works most of the time with one-to-one interviews. Avoid it in a debate.

2) If you must answer it, without having an answer, you can restate the question and then take the conversation in a different direction.

3) You can sidestep the question completely by not addressing the question and restating your key messages. Never guess or give an answer that you think is right because you will regret it. If you don't know the answer or don't want to answer a question, DONT! Never say no comment. This could be interpreted as guilt. Go back to a talking point. They may ask you "why don't you answer the question?" You can reply by saying "I did answer

the question." Remember the media is looking to corner and exploit every word. As you speak, this should always stay top of mind.

Avoid Rhetorical Arguments (until you know how to use them to your advantage)

I have learned that arguing with liberals is futile. In a debate, the left will want to pull you into their world of rhetorical arguments that go round and round. A world where common sense has been exiled and ambiguity reigns supreme. The left has an advantage here because liberalism is not defined. Conservatives live by a code of clearly defined morals. Liberals believe in situational ethics where guilt could be innocence and innocence could be guilt. This depends on who did the offense, whether or not they were rich or poor, white or black, man or woman, young or old, gay or straight etc. Liberal morality fluctuates.

It benefits them to pull you into an argument where ethics are defined by emotions instead of some type of uniform standard. Leftist propaganda is based on exploiting emotions. This is why they will focus on intent. You have to focus on results. Conservatives win when they articulate the practical application of conservative values. Liberalism/Socialism/ Communism has always led to oppression and misery wherever it has been tried. Liberals will argue that the government should provide free healthcare because it's unfair for a parent to worry about their child not having coverage. Conservatives will argue that a parent would rather have a good paying job and pay for affordable healthcare coverage instead of being unemployed and getting it for free. Rhetorical arguments are designed to be monotonous and eternal. I don't engage. Stay pragmatic.

Liberals only represent about 20% of the views in this country whereas Conservatives and moderates represent 77% (roughly 42% Conservative.)[79] If you are a conservative having a political conversation, the chances are you'll be arguing with the 20% that you're not going to ever convince to see otherwise. Most people tend to shy away from political arguments. Liberals are a vocal minority that happen to be in control of a majority of the media. However the overwhelming majority of their viewers agree with you. So you have to speak to the people through your liberal counterpart. Remember your objective is to convince the audience to see the merits of your perspective and not convert a liberal to conservatism.

On the other hand, the liberal is out to convert your thinking along with everyone else's because they thrive on control. The left operates based on groupthink for the masses with the consolidation of power at the top. They are out to control the actions of the people whereas you are out to persuade people to take control of themselves. They don't like intellectual debate so you can expect that they are going to call you a racist, homophobe, bigot, hypocrite and anything else they can think of. This is as constant as gravity. Deal with it.

Take the opportunity to debate a liberal as a gift so that you can force them to explain their positions. Make them look irrational. Get them to reveal their intentions. Liberals are masters at masking their intentions with feel-good rhetoric. Force them to reveal how they benefit from their plans. Force them to admit to financial gain. Make them argue the merits of welfare and explain why they don't personally receive government handouts but they claim that they great for other people. Ask them to explain why they are successful and the people they advocate for aren't. Ask them why they don't live in government housing but suggest others should be content with it. Have them explain that if wealth is so evil, why don't all of these wealthy Liberals divest their resources and spread it around to the people they "fight" for.

Never Repeat The Reporters Negative Comment!

CBS Anchor Katie Couric's interview with Alaska Governor and Vice Presidential candidate Sarah Palin is a prime example. The interview took place at the start of the recent economic downturn and refers to the then proposed $700 billion dollar government bailout. Couric asked: If this doesn't pass, do you think there's a risk of another Great Depression?" To which Palin responded: "Unfortunately, that is the road that America may find itself on. Not necessarily this, as it's been proposed, has to pass or we're gonna find ourselves in another Great Depression. But there has to be action taken, bipartisan effort—Congress not pointing fingers at this point at...one another, but finding the solution to this, taking action and being serious about the reforms on Wall Street that are needed."[80]

Here are some of the headlines from the next day:
"Palin Warns Depression May Be Looming"
"Sarah Palin Depression Fears"
"Palin Says Another Great Depression Possible"

By repeating the interviewers negative (Great Depression), Palin attached herself to the negative and it became hers. If there is one absolute in the being at the other end of a microphone or camera, it's this. **Never Repeat The Reporters' Negative Comment![81]**

First of all, we all knew that Couric would do her best to make Palin leave the interview looking unfavorable. However, there were a few things that Palin could have done to mitigate some of the media's intent to embarrass her. Accepting a negative premise erodes your message. Even though you may not agree, it may appear that you do. By repeating their negative argument, you take ownership of it. When you don't accept the premise, make sure that you clearly state your objection before answering the question. Sometimes you have to sidestep the question. Sidestepping is addressing parts of the question without really answering it. You don't refuse answering a question because the audience will think that you are lying or incompetent. This is more art than science so it takes time and practice to develop. Your goal is to leave the audience felling you are confident and knowledgeable.[82]

Beware of reporters who offer multiple choice questions. "is this a recession...or the worst market collapse ever?" Either answer is a negative response. Come up with a positive response. Use a bridge phrase to get to the message you want to deliver. "Katie, the real issue is what do we do to improve the economy? Our campaign has a plan to cut taxes, put more cash back into consumers pockets and put financial police back on the job to clean up Wall Street. Practice your positive responses before each interview. You have to accentuate the positive, eliminate the negative and stay far away from Mr. In-Between.[83]

Here is another good contrast of how conservatives should handle situations where they are faced with negative premises or negative accusations. During the 2010 elections Republican Senate candidates Rand Paul (Kentucky) and Christine O'Donnell (Delaware) faced accusations of indiscretions from their youth from anonymous sources. If the media had any integrity, this would have never been an issue but they don't. Many of them aim to destroy conservatives at all costs.

During the Kentucky Senate race of 2010 Democratic nominee Jack Conway ran ads accusing Republican nominee Rand Paul of alleged college shenanigans in hopes of convincing Kentucky voters to support him. The ad features a story about an alleged hazing incident Paul participated in as an undergraduate at Baylor. According to an anonymous woman who says she was a student when Paul attended the school, Paul and a friend tied her up, put her in a creek and asked her to pray to "Aqua Buddha." The alleged incident was part of Paul's membership in a student group called the NoZe brotherhood that was banned from the Baptist-backed Baylor campus for "mocking Christianity."[84]

Instead of acknowledging any of this, Paul stuck to his message, never addressing any of the accusations from the anonymous source. Conway pounded Paul with ads and during debate with these accusations. Paul could've easily gotten frustrated and said "I never did that." Had he done that, which is what the media wanted, it would have opened a new can of worms. Paul would have been taken ownership of the accusations regardless of its validity. Conway said the ad was intended to show Paul's history of questionable decision making, a view he attempted to tie to his attacks on Paul's history as a political pundit and candidate. Paul said the ad was an attack on his faith -- Paul is a Christian -- and said that Kentucky voters would be turned off by the spot. After the ads, Paul increased his polling advantage to double digits, and eventually won the election. This is a great example of not accepting accusations and staying on message.

On the other hand, Republican Delaware Senate Candidate Christine O'Donnell was accused of engaging in witchcraft during her early 20s. Perhaps it was an act of self-discovery as many people experiment with activities that they will later regret during that age. Whether it was true or not she should have never addressed it. When you address negative assertions, you give them credibility. But O'Donnell didn't stop there. She created a defensive ad where she stated "I'm not a witch," she says in the ad, with piano music playing in the background. "I'm nothing you've heard. I'm you." This was just plain weird and had no place in the messaging for a successful campaign. She said in an interview on ABC's "Good Morning America" that she regretted releasing the ad saying that the intention to "kill" the witchcraft commentary, but it backfired.[85]

The addressing issues head-on logic may work in the real world, but not in the media. You have to realize that the media is a different animal. Things with no real-world value can be created and blown out of proportion in the media. O'Donnell's misstep was parodied on "Saturday Night Live" and all over the Internet. She not only provided fuel for her opponents, she allowed people that may not have cared about politics to assassinate her character for fun. Unfortunately Christine didn't win her Senate bid.

Keep in mind that the media is not your friend. Never get cozy with reporters because their job is not to be your friend. Perhaps the most grotesque example of the lack of humanity of liberal reporters was when MSNBC's Norah O'Donnell grilled a teenage girl, waiting in line to meet Sarah Palin, as though she was a congressional candidate. To no surprise, O'Donnell an experienced journalist, got the better of the kid in a political discussion. She asked the girl about Palin's position on the financial bailout and surprisingly the kid was not well-versed in Palin's economic platform.[86] Apparently this episode was a triumph for the liberal movement because it was blasted all over the Internet, and ran several times in the mainstream media echo chamber.

O'Donnell seemed pleasured by besting a kid about specifics of federal economic policy. I would love to see her go on BET and ask some of the million dollar rappers that supported Obama some of the same detailed policy questions. I would love to see her give a pop quiz at the Oscars and see how many random Liberals can answer specific questions about Obama's two years in office. I am sure that many of them would be stumped like that kid was. The video was posted on YouTube by the worthless people at Media Matters as a victory for liberalism.[87]

If they are willing to do this to a kid, no conservative is safe. Many Liberals in the media are unscrupulous when it comes to their desire to destroy conservatives regardless of their age, experience, or education level. Their marching orders are clear, so it's up to you to be prepared. Preserving and perpetuating leftist narratives is their objective. It really doesn't matter if you think it is fair or not because the game has been the same for generations. Your objective is to defend freedom, our American way of life and the Constitution. However, you can't avoid the media because the only way to reach a massive audience is through them because they have the means. However, by adopting the recommendations in this book, and practicing the exercises that follow, you will be better equipped to engage the main stream media.

7
Exercises

Decoding Headlines

Here are actual headlines. Pretend that you are a casual observer of the news. You are not affiliated with any political organization, and have no particular voting pattern. You live a busy life working raising your family and attending religious services. When you occasionally read the newspaper, you only read the headlines and perhaps the first few sentences.

Below are some headlines from major news organizations. The headlines are from news stories. None of the headlines are from editorials or opinions.

Directions:
1. Read each headline and first paragraph.
2. Using assumptions based on the information given decide:
    - What do you think is the main idea of the story?
    - As a reader, how does the headline make you feel?
    - Do you think the writer is sending a political message?
    - Is the writer is favorable or unfavorable to the subject?
    - Is the story used to support one group and undermine another?
    - From what vantage point do you think the headline was written (neutral, liberal or conservative)?
    - Based on what you know or assume, do you think the headline accurately depicts the situation?
    - Can you create a headline from an opposing point of view and or a neutral position?

Headline: Senate GOP again kills extension of unemployment benefits[88]

Source: The Los Angeles Times

Date: July 1, 2010

1st Paragraph: WASHINGTON — For the third time in as many weeks, Senate Republicans on Wednesday successfully filibustered a bill to continue providing unemployment checks to millions of people who have been collecting benefits for more than six months. But this time, the slimmed-down measure attracted two Republican votes, so its passage seems assured once a replacement fills the seat of Sen. Robert C. Byrd (D-W.Va.), who died Monday.

Headline: Obama Hails Vote on Health Care as Answering 'the Call of History'[89]

Source: New York Times

Date: March 21, 2010

1st Paragraph: WASHINGTON — House Democrats approved a far-reaching overhaul of the nation's health system on Sunday, voting over unanimous Republican opposition to provide medical coverage to tens of millions of uninsured Americans after an epic political battle that could define the differences between the parties for years. With the 219-to-212 vote, the House gave final approval to legislation passed by the Senate on Christmas Eve. Thirty-four Democrats joined Republicans in voting against the bill. The vote sent the measure to President Obama, whose yearlong push for the legislation has been the centerpiece of his agenda and a test of his political power.

Headline: Republicans target Democrats on healthcare reform[90]

Source: Reuters

Date: Mar 23, 2010

1st Paragraph: WASHINGTON- Vulnerable Democratic U.S. lawmakers who backed President Barack Obama's healthcare reform plan are being targeted with freshly cut Republican TV attack ads. The spots hope to convince voters that the landmark healthcare measure, which narrowly won final congressional approval on Sunday, is a bad idea and that the lawmakers who supported it should be defeated in the November election. "After all this wheeling and dealing, we still have a cost-raising, tax-increasing bill," an announcer says in one of a number of ads by the House Republican campaign committee set to begin airing this week. "Stop the madness."

Headline: Obama calls for federal wage freeze[91]

Source: CNN

Date: November 29, 2010

1st Paragraph: NEW YORK (CNNMoney.com) -- President Obama on Monday called for a two-year freeze in the wages of federal employees. The freeze, which would need congressional approval and save $60 billion over 10 years, would make a small dent in the nation's debt problem. Budget experts say nearly $6 trillion in deficit reduction is needed to stabilize the debt, so the new proposal achieves less than 1% of what's ultimately needed.

Headline: Democrats chip away at GOP on financial reform[92]

Source: Reuters

Date: Apr 16, 2010

1st Paragraph: To get financial reform legislation through the U.S. Senate, Democrats need to peel away just one Republican to support their sweeping bill. To improve their odds, they are courting a handful of moderate Republicans, some of whom face reelection challenges, and some from states hit hard by recession and foreclosures, according to Senate aides, analysts and lobbyists. Democrats want reforms to tighten bank and capital market regulation to prevent a repeat of the 2007-2009 financial crisis that tipped the economy into a deep recession. Most Republicans say the reforms represent a costly over-reach of government. But some have sought compromise on reforms to prevent future debacles like the Bush administration's 2008 bailout of AIG and the Lehman Brothers bankruptcy.

Headline: Republicans (and One Democrat) Block Debate on Financial Reform Bill[93]

Source: CBS News

Date: April 26, 2010

1st Paragraph: Senate Republicans held together Monday afternoon to block efforts by Democrats to officially begin debate on the financial industry reform bill. No Republicans cast a "yes" vote on the procedural motion, keeping Democrats from the 60 vote threshold needed to move forward. One Democrat, Nebraska's Ben Nelson, voted "no" outright. The vote was 57-41. Two Republicans did not vote: Utah's Bob Bennett and Missouri's Kit Bond. Senate Majority Leader Harry Reid switched his vote to a "no" so that he can bring the bill back to the floor, something he is vowing to do that later this week.

Headline: President Obama slams obstructionist Republicans at GOP issues retreat [94]

Source: New York Daily News

Date: January 30, 2010

1st Paragraph: WASHINGTON - President Obama dove headfirst into the belly of the GOP beast Friday - and left the not-so-loyal opposition bleeding on a Baltimore ballroom floor. He skewered Republicans for obstructionist tactics, dubious facts and a lack of civility in opposing his domestic agenda, especially health care reform. "If you were to listen to the debate and, frankly, how some of you went after this bill, you'd think that this thing was some Bolshevik plot," Obama told the GOP issues retreat after unveiling a proposal for $33 billion in small-business tax incentives. House Republican leaders had tried to score political points by inviting Obama to their lair. Problem was, he showed up.

Headline: Obama tells GOP it's bad time for 'no' as meetings with Republicans loom[95]
Source: New York Daily News
Date: November 15, 2010
1st Paragraph: Ahead of his meeting with the Republican leaders this week, President Obama on Sunday warned them the era of just say no is over. The GOP opposed nearly every initiative Obama and the Democrats offered - and sometimes passed - over the last two years. They were so successful at casting those policies as job-killing bailouts that were deadly to the economy that voters on Election Day still believed - by a 2-to-1 margin - that the economy was shrinking, bailouts were ongoing and their taxes were heading up - even though the opposite was true. With the GOP gaining greater say in the Senate and taking over the House, Obama said they'd have to play the game differently over the next two years.

Headline: The GOP House's Opening Act: Making a Statement or Making a Mockery?[96]
Source: Time Magazine
Date: January 5, 2011
1st Paragraph: Two months after a sweeping victory in the midterm elections, Republicans will officially reclaim the House of Representatives on Wednesday. But before the new majority party begins the business of governing — which it doesn't even really get down to until the end of the month — it will take the opportunity to savor it's triumph and make a statement with a good dose of Washington political theater.

107

At about noon, the House clerk will call the chamber to order. After reciting a prayer and the Pledge of Allegiance, the members will elect Representative John Boehner as Speaker. The Ohioan will be presented by his predecessor, outgoing Democratic Speaker Nancy Pelosi, before swearing in the largest GOP freshman class in more than half a century.

Headline: Recitation of Constitution set in House renews debate over Founders' intentions[97]

Source: Washington Post

Date: January 4, 2011

1st Paragraph: And the Founders said: Let there be a constitution. And the Founders looked at the articles and clauses and saw that it was good.

For more than 200 years, Americans have revered the Constitution as the law of the land, but the GOP and Tea Party heralding of the document in recent months - and the planned recitation on the House floor Thursday - has caused some Democrats to worry that the charter is being misconstrued as the immutable word of God. "They are reading it like a sacred text," said New York Rep. Jerrold Nadler (D-N.Y.), the outgoing chairman of the House Judiciary subcommittee on the Constitution, Civil Rights and Civil Liberties, who has studied and memorized the Constitution with talmudic intensity.

Headline: Democrats Try to Crack Mystery of the Missing Voters[98]

Source: Wall Street Journal

Date: November 23, 2010

1st Paragraph: A popular theory of this year's midterm election holds that Democrats took a shellacking in part because big chunks of the party's core liberal base, discouraged at the path of the Obama administration, stayed home rather than show up to vote as they did in 2008. It's an interesting narrative. It also doesn't appear to be entirely accurate. WSJ's Jerry Seib discusses voter turnout in the midterm election, and why a large chunk of no-shows were moderate Democrats in the center who turned out for Obama in 2008 but not in 2010. While it's correct that some key parts of the Democratic coalition—young voters and African-Americans among them—didn't perform as they did in 2008, evidence emerging as the dust settles from this month's election suggests the bigger hole in the side of the Democratic ship came from moderates in the political center who didn't show up. (Those absences were in addition to the wave of independent swing voters also from the center who, exit polls showed, turned out but switched their votes to the Republicans.)

Headline: Promises, promises: GOP drops some out of the gate[99]
Source: Associated Press
Date: January 6, 2011
1st Paragraph: WASHINGTON (AP) —Republicans have already violated some of the vows they made in taking stewardship of the House. Their pledge to cut $100 billion from the budget in one year won't be kept. The first spending cut measure to come to the floor — imposing a 5 percent spending cut on lawmakers' budgets for office expenses and staff salaries — is hardly in keeping with the promise to return spending back to pre-Obama levels. Such costs have risen by 14 percent since that time. And for a coming vote seeking to repeal the health care overhaul, the first major initiative of the new Congress, lawmakers won't be allowed to propose changes to the legislation despite Republican promises to end such heavy-handed tactics from the days of Democratic control.

Headline: Anonymous donors spent $132M on 2010 campaign ads[100]
Source: MSNBC
Date: January 10, 2010
1st Paragraph: NEW YORK — Independent groups that do not disclose the identity of their donors spent $132.5 million to influence elections nationwide this year, accounting for about a third of all spending by

outside groups in the 2010 election cycle, a report released Friday found. The analysis by the office of New York City Public Advocate Bill de Blasio aimed to quantify how federal campaigns had been affected by the Supreme Court's so-called Citizens United ruling. The ruling, handed down in January, cleared the way for companies and labor unions to spend unlimited funds to influence elections, often using money from anonymous donors. Groups including the U.S. Chamber of Commerce and the American Federation of State, County and Municipal Employees took advantage of the new rules, spending tens of millions on campaign ads in races across the country.

Headline: Obama exhorts Republicans to put politics aside[101]

Source: ABC News

Date: January 4, 2011

1st Paragraph: Ending a two-week vacation, President Barack Obama is appealing to newly-empowered Republicans to resist jockeying for the White House in 2012 and work with him to get the economy growing and the jobless back to work. Facing anything but a political soft landing after his holiday stay in Hawaii, Obama told reporters en route to the capital Tuesday that he understands Republicans, who recaptured the House in last fall's elections, "are going to play to their base for a certain period of time." "But I'm pretty confident that they're going to recognize that our job is to govern and make sure that we are delivering jobs for the American people and that we are creating a competitive economy for the 21st century," the President said. Marine One, with Obama, Michelle Obama, and daughters Malia and Sasha aboard, landed on the White House lawn about 11:30, following a nine-hour flight on Air Force One from Hawaii.

Headline: David Letterman Made Fun of Philanderers For Years as he Pursued Own Affairs[102]

110

Source: Fox News

Date: October 7, 2009

1st Paragraph: Turns out David Letterman doesn't just live on a TV show. He also lives in a glass house, where for years he's hurled comedy zingers at misbehaving politicians, even as he brashly engaged in hanky-panky of his own. In March 2008, Letterman was taking potshots at Eliot Spitzer, then governor of New York, who was embroiled in an investigation into a high-end prostitution ring. "It's so sunny and bright outside that, earlier today, Eliot Spitzer came out of a brothel squinting," Letterman cracked in a monologue.

Headline: In Black Belt: McCain wins hearts not votes[103]

Source: The Birmingham News

Date: April 22, 2008

1st Paragraph: GEE'S BEND - Seventy-two-year-old Mary Lee Bendolph beamed as she took Sen. John McCain's hand, welcoming the would-be president to her poor but proud community isolated on three sides by the brown waters of the Alabama River. Together she, McCain and the other members of Bendolph's group of old friends, known to the world as the quilters of Gee's Bend, walked onto the new ferry that connects this community of descendants of slaves to the rest of the county. During the ride across the river, the group sang Gospel songs and took turns having their photos made with the Republican presumptive nominee for the White House. McCain's ride across the Alabama was the highlight of a day in which he went to places that Republicans seldom visit and that he said too often are forgotten by too many Americans.

Headline: Pelosi: Incoming Speaker Boehner 'Known to Cry'[104]

Source: Fox News

Date: November 20, 2010

111

1st Paragraph: Outgoing Speaker Nancy Pelosi may be giving up the gavel to Rep. John Boehner in the next Congress but she hinted this week that she still wears the pants in the House. In an interview with The New York Times on Thursday, Pelosi highlighted her successor's softer side when asked if she saw him tear up on election night as he addressed his supporters after Republicans captured the House.

Headline: Immigration Vote Leaves Obama's Policy in Disarray[105]
Source: The New York Times
Date: December 18, 2010
1st Paragraph: The vote by the Senate on Saturday to block a bill to grant legal status to hundreds of thousands of illegal immigrant students was a painful setback to an emerging movement of immigrants and also appeared to leave the immigration policy of the Obama administration, which has supported the bill and the movement, in disarray. The bill, known as the Dream Act, gained 55 votes in favor with 41 against, a tally short of the 60 votes needed to bring it to the floor for debate. Five Democrats broke ranks to vote against the bill, while only three Republicans voted for it. The defeat in the Senate came after the House of Representatives passed the bill last week.

Headline: How Wall St. Execs bankrolled GOP victory[106]
Source: MSNBC
Date: January 5, 2011
1st Paragraph: A small network of hedge fund executives pumped at least $10 million into Republican campaign committees and allied groups before November's elections, helping bankroll GOP victories that this week will change the balance of power in Washington, according to a review of campaign records and interviews with industry insiders by the Center for Public Integrity and NBC News. Bitterly opposed to President Barack Obama's economic and regulatory policies — including proposals

112

to increase taxes on some of their profits — top Wall Street hedge fund moguls were unusually energized during last year's election. They held multiple fundraisers and coordinated strategy to direct what appear to be unprecedented sums into the coffers of GOP and allied political committees, according to industry and GOP fundraising sources.

Headline: Is Darrell Issa the new Joe McCarthy?[107]
Source: The Washington Post
Date: January 5, 2011
1st Paragraph: To the victors in the congressional elections goes the power of subpoena, as Rep. Darrell Issa (R-Calif.) has been so eager to remind the Democrats. But as the new Congress is seated, Issa and his GOP colleagues should note the difference between investigation and witch-hunt. Too often in our political history, the former has turned into the latter. It was scary, frankly, to hear Issa describe the executive branch under President Obama as "one of the most corrupt administrations." What on earth was he talking about? This is an administration that has often tied itself in knots with petty ethical rules. Issa's comment bordered on demagogy.

Headline: Minorities ride GOP wave to groundbreaking wins[108]
Source: Associated Press
Date: November 3, 2011
1st Paragraph: WASHINGTON – The Republican wave produced groundbreaking results for minority candidates, from Latina and Indian-American governors to a pair of black congressmen from the Deep South. In New Mexico, Susana Martinez was elected as the nation's first female Hispanic governor. Nikki Haley, whose parents were born in India, will be the first woman governor in South Carolina, and Brian Sandoval became Nevada's first Hispanic governor. Insurance company owner Tim Scott will be the first black Republican congressman from South Carolina

113

since Reconstruction, after easily winning in his conservative district. Scott, a 45-year-old state representative, earned a primary victory over the son of the one-time segregationist U.S. Sen. Strom Thurmond.

Media Interviews
Role Play

For these exercises, you need two people. One will act as a politician and the other as reporter. For each scenario there will be a summary of the situation, the position of the politician and the information sought by the reporter. The situation is one that is very controversial that the public needs to be informed about. Remember that both have different motivations and goals. The politician is seeking to control the narrative and give the appearance that he/she is in control of the situation. He only wants to provide a minimal amount of details. The reporter is seeking to provide his reporters with specifics. Conduct a 3-5 minute interview. After you conduct the first interview switch positions and do it again.

If possible record a video. Then watch it to critique your performances. Who was the most effective at achieving their goal? How could you improve your performance? Was there a clear winner? Describe your thought process. Were you quick to answer questions, did you hesitate or were you talking at a comfortable pace? Were you searching for the right words, were you totally candid, or on message and in control? Use your imagination. Have fun!

Before the role play interview begins:

<u>Reporter/Journalist:</u>	Identify a few key leading questions that can help achieve your objectives.
<u>Interviewee:</u>	Take a few moments to create your message track with 3-5 key messages.

Political Interviews

Political interviews are different from information interviews (i.e. grand opening of a new bowling alley or an upcoming concert) because they tend to be adversarial. Politicians are famous for avoiding questions and doubletalk. They also do their best to present themselves as being in control of the situation even when it is clearly out of hand. Politicians deal with situations much different than most citizens. In most cases their livelihood depends on convincing large groups of people with different motivations to freely vote for them. They are routinely faced with seemingly no-win situations. They have to constantly juggle issues and language in order to get elected and stay in office. However, most people have the luxury of being forthright without having to answer to the electorate.

This exercise is designed to help you understand the thought process of a politician and a journalist. As the politician, you will be asked about situations that will challenge your authority and loyalties. You will have to use your language skills to convince the public that you are in charge of the situation. As the reporter, your job is to push the politician into answering some tough questions. You know that they will do their best to dodge them so you have to be creative with your questioning.

Situation #1: Things are getting really tense in a blue-collar town. The town's economy is supported primarily by a local factory and union. The mayor and his supporters on City Council are sponsoring legislation to make his city a sanctuary city for illegal immigrants because there is an increasing number moving to the community. Although the union and community have been very supportive of this mayor and his party for many years, they are now threatening to support the opposition. Other citizens in the community are appalled by the legislation as well. Civil

Rights and Immigrant rights groups praise the legislation as a step in the right direction to bring justice and equality to a community that badly needs to move forward on race relations. Many longtime citizens believe that the influx of illegal immigrants is the cause behind increased crime and much of the city's financial burden. The mayor argues that becoming a sanctuary city will be a benefit for the community in many ways.

Politician: Control the narrative! You want to maintain support from the unions and solicit support from illegal immigrant groups. You believe in amnesty for illegals but to have made your viewpoint made publicly will be political suicide. You are trying to appease two groups with opposing points of view.

Reporter: Your goal is to get the mayor to admit whether or not he supports amnesty for illegals. You want him to admit that he is pandering to illegal immigrants. The community wants to know whose side he is on.

Situation #2: For decades, residents of the predominantly African-American Jackson Heights neighborhood inside of one of America's largest and most liberal cities have spent their summers having barbecues, playing football games and enjoying outdoor fun during the summer months at what's now known as Martin Luther King, Jr. Park. It has significant historical value because it was the only public park for black people prior to integration. Recently, an environmental group discovered that a rare form of earthworm native to the area is about to become extinct. The worm is important to the local ecosystem. The largest concentration of this earthworm lives in the most frequented areas of MLK Park. A group of very politically influential and well-funded environmental groups have demanded that the park be shutdown immediately in order to preserve the earthworm and protect the ecosystem. The civil rights community has led protests and demonstrations in order to save the park. You are the mayor of this town. Roughly ninety percent of the African-American voting community has voted for your party in every election for several generations. These environmental groups have supported your party financially for generations. Both groups agree that there will be no compromise. They both believe that their loyalty to your party is enough persuasion to see things their way. With the election around the corner, the environmentalists have withheld their funding until they get a decision. The political opposition is growing in fund raising and support. The media wants to know what you're going to do.

Politician: Control the narrative! You want to maintain support from the environmentalists and the African-Americans. You are falling behind on fund raising and in the polls. You need money fast.

Reporter: Your goal is to find out if the mayor is going to close the park or not. You want to know which constituency is more important.

Situation #3: You are a member of a five-member City Council preparing to run for mayor. Your party has a 3-2 to advantage on the Council and the mayor is from the opposing party. There is a big real estate deal on the table for the city that could provide thousands of jobs and an economic boom which your city is badly in need of. The developer said that if the deal isn't closed in the next few weeks, they will accept the bid from another city. The mayor has been trying to seal the deal for years and now things are finally about to happen. The other two Council members from your party oppose the plan for political reasons. They can afford to do so because they represent "safe" districts. Polls show that roughly 60% of voters support the development; however, your political base – among the remaining 40% – adamantly opposes the development. With unemployment rising, the city could use these jobs now.

Politician: Control the narrative! Everyone knows that you are preparing to run for mayor but you haven't announced yet. You don't want your campaign for mayor to have anything to do with this situation. If you support the development, the mayor could look like a hero and ride into reelection. If you vote against it, a majority of the city will be upset and remember it in the fall. You don't want to look like an obstructionist but you do want to appear as though you support economic development.

Reporter: Your goal is to find out what the councilman is going to do. You want to know which constituency is more important. You want to know if his mayoral aspirations will have any affect on his decision-making process?

Situation #4: A wealthy socialite and behind-the-scenes political dealmaker was just charged with sexual deviance. He's being accused of creating raunchy porn with underage girls, and some of them are illegal immigrants. You are a sitting member of Congress. Presently you are in a tough race for the Senate. You have a slight lead in the polls. Throughout your career he has always been there to pull strings and deliver the funding that you needed as you ascended in the political world. You have made a career running on a family values platform. He has answered every call and put up the money you needed to stay elected. Now he really needs you. Influential party bosses, the general public and of course your opponent have been pressuring you to condemn him. You have been able to avoid the topic but you can't do it any longer. The socialite has promised to use his influence to eliminate all funding from you if you cannot stand by him in his time need. The election is less than two months away.

Politician: Control the narrative! You are in a tight race and can't afford to lose any funding. At this point in the campaign you can't find enough new donors to make up for the potential loss of his influence. You were heavily favored to maintain the seat, but the longer you remain silent, the more your opponent gains in the polls and fund-raising.

Reporter: Your goal is to find out what he's going to do. You want to know if he is going to make a decision based on political expediency or the moral standards he has touted for years.

Situation #5: You are a Commissioner in a Southern state of a predominantly rural county. All of a sudden you find yourself as the subject of a worldwide media sensation. While your county is relatively obscure and at least 200 miles from the closest urban area, civil rights groups and media have descended in your once quiet county. When a new resident of the county visited the county office he discovered pictures from the Civil War that he found offensive and outdated. After his attempt to have them removed he sought help from national civil rights organizations. They are now protesting in the county. These protests are disrupting normal county operations. The community overwhelmingly supports leaving the pictures where they are because they believe they represent their heritage. Your voters and county are solidly behind your decision to keep the pictures. Outside groups are pressuring you to remove the pictures as well as the governor and members of your party. However, the county economy is dependent on the manufacturing facility. The corporate office, based in San Francisco, made the statement that refusal to remove the pictures will result in the loss of the plant. You have accepted an interview from a major network television news organization.

Politician: Control the narrative! You have been a long time public servant in the county and have no desire for higher office. However the party bosses have told you in private that the party could suffer statewide because of this. The party has been very supportive of you through the years. The people of the county have supported you and trust that you would do the right thing and stand by them as you always have.

Reporter: Your goal is to find out what he's going to do.

Situation #6: You are the mayor of a Midwestern city struggling to make it through the economic recession. As part of your campaign platform you promised to make your city attractive to big-time movie producers as a way to improve the arts community as well as become a form of economic development. Your investments in the idea have not paid off until now. A major Hollywood studio would like to film a movie in your town for six months. This could provide the economic boom you are looking for in addition to possibly securing future projects. The problem is, the movie is based on a very controversial book that contains polarizing subjects. The studio would obviously need to film in public places and display graphic material. The city's voters, as well as your political party, are split on the issue. Your base is not supportive of the movie but the opposing party is.

Politician: Control the narrative! You are term limited and two years from leaving office. You have been preparing to run for Congress. This is an issue that will definitely come into play. You have sacrificed a great deal of political capital in order to attract moviemakers to your city. This could be a big part of your legacy. You support the project but don't want to alienate your base. While the opposition party is supportive of you on this issue, you know they won't be there when it's election time. You are going to need your base during the primary because you will be challenging a formidable County Commissioner.

Reporter: Your goal is to find out what he's going to do. You want to know if he is going to make a decision based on his desire to run for Congress or the economic needs of the city. You want to know what's more important having a legacy as one of the city's great mayors or potentially securing a seat in Congress.

Propaganda Interviews

These situations are designed so that you can speak from the position of an activist with a well-defined perspective. You will be defending your position while being interview by an opinion journalist (i.e. Sean Hannity or Chris Matthews) with well-defined opposing views. The audience primarily consists of people with views contrary to yours.

The purpose of this exercise is to teach you how to defend your position by answering questions from an opposing perspective. Most interviews will not be friendly, so you need to be ready to defend your position at any time.

Situation #1: You are the leader of a local Tea Party group. Your group has been very active over the last year and your membership has grown to over 300 members. Each of your rallies has attracted at least 2000 people. Someone that claimed to be one of your members, whom you don't know personally, was quoted in the news with a statement that has been interpreted as racist. The statement was "we are taking our country back from a man who wasn't even born here." The local news media is taking this opportunity to connect your Tea Party group with racism. You now have been asked to do several interviews in the local market.

Tea Party Leader: Control the narrative! You don't even know this guy. You have no record of him ever coming to a meeting. You personally believe this could be a plant but have no proof. You have to defend your constitutional beliefs and convince the audience that your group is not racist.

Opinion Journalist: You host a prominent liberal radio show. There is a lot of pressure being put on the local Tea Party because of the situation. You want to press them on the race issue to get them to admit to being racist or make a comment that can be interpreted as racist. You believe some members of the Tea Party are connected to extreme racist groups.

Situation #2: You are the president of a local civil liberties group. You just sued the county commission and won! As a result, convicted sex offenders are allowed to live anywhere in the county and no longer have to be listed on the county's website. Before the ruling, convicted sex offenders had to live in restricted areas and be tracked on a website. You believe that this is a victory for individual rights while local parent groups are outraged. Many in the community feel that children are now in danger all over the county.

Civil Liberties leader: Control the narrative! You believe that preserving individual civil liberties is the most sacred thing in our republic. You are working to convince the audience that defending the dignity and privacy of these individuals will enhance the community in the long run.

Opinion Journalist: You are a prominent conservative talk show host. You believe that the county has the duty to protect citizens and especially our children from convicted sexual offenders. You want to pressure the civil liberties leader into admitting that they care more about sex offenders than they do children.

Situation #3: You are the president of a local civil liberties group. You are defending a man convicted of breaking in to a home and killing and raping the mother and two daughters and leaving the father to die. The father survived the attack. There is a massive public outcry to give this man the death penalty. You believe that he should get life imprisonment instead.

Civil Liberties leader: Control the narrative! You believe that preserving individual civil liberties is the most sacred thing in our republic. You disagree with capital punishment and believe that life imprisonment is a much worse penalty. You are working to convince the audience that our society will be just as barbaric as the offender if we kill him because killing him won't bring back the victims.

Opinion Journalist: You are prominent conservative talk show host. You believe that the offender should be put to death as soon as possible in order to bring closure to the father. You want to pressure the civil liberties leader into admitting that they care more about violent offenders than they do innocent victims.

Situation #4: A local conservation group is pressuring the government to shut down a local manufacturer because they believe that the waste from their facility is resulting in poor air quality and contributing to global warming. The plant is one of the biggest economic contributors to the area. To lose it will be a big blow to the economy. The local conservation group believe that the facility can be converted into the manufacture of "green" products and significantly diminish the community's carbon footprint. They would like the government to use its influence to either convince the business to leave or create sanctions that will force them to leave. The workers and their families believe that the plant should stay since the effects on the environment are allegedly minimal.

Environmentalist leader: Control the narrative! You believe that the biggest issue facing our world is global warming and its effect on our climate. It is important that we be stewards of the environment and that the loss of economic output is a necessary sacrifice to preserve the health planet. You want to convince the audience that once the plant reopens as a manufacturer of green products, the jobs in the community will be restored. Although it may take 2-5 years, it is a worthy sacrifice for our future.

Opinion Journalist: You are a prominent conservative talk show host. You don't believe in global warming at all. You believe that this is just a scam in order to redistribute wealth to leaders of the liberal agenda with no concern over the people that will be the most affected. You want to pressure them to admit that they don't care about private property. You want to know why they believe that the government should force this company out of business.

Situation #5: You are the leader of a prominent pro-life group. Due your efforts, one of the largest abortion clinics in the country was closed in one of the city's inner-city neighborhoods. Your group was able to prove that some of the practices of the clinic were illegal, and for the past several years, your group has offered free prenatal care to any woman that walks into your doors. The abortion facility's closure has resulted in many civil rights and pro-choice groups making claims that women in the inner-city are being forced to pay for "back alley" abortions which are unsanitary and potentially deadly for mother and child. They also are accusing your group of forcing women to raise children they can't afford, and thus forcing undue financial burdens on the government.

Pro-life leader: Control the narrative! You believe that abortion is morally wrong and that as a society we should protect the unborn. In addition to prenatal services, your group offers ongoing parenting classes and other support to help people develop healthy family relationships.

Opinion Journalist: You are the host of a prominent liberal talk show. You and your audience believe that this group is hypocritical and has no right to force this facility into closure. You admit that there may have been a couple of mistakes but nothing worthy of closure. You believe that women have the right to do whatever they want to their bodies. You have been told that poor and minority women are now suffering having to get "back alley" abortions when they could have gone to this facility for professional care. You want this group to take responsibility for the poor health decisions being forced on poor and minority women.

Situation #6: You are a prominent minister and longtime civil rights leader in the local African-American community. You are also the outgoing president of the local chapter of the oldest national civil rights organization. A group of African-American boys were recently involved in a fight in a suburban high school. African-Americans comprise about 10% of the student population. Five African-American boys are accused of jumping two White boys. As a result, roughly 10-15 White boys joined the fight against the five African-American boys. No one was hurt. Witnesses say the fight started because of building racial tension and that one of the African-Americans started the fight. Police reports state that all five African-American boys provoked the altercation. All five African American boys were expelled and two of the White boys received three-day suspensions. Local and national civil rights groups have traveled to the school to protest and march. Community leaders are pressuring the district to create a director and a board to monitor racial issues.

Civil rights leader: Control the narrative! You believe that the African-American boys were treated unfairly and deserve the same punishment as the two White boys. You also believe that more of the boys involved in the fight should be disciplined. You believe that it is your duty as an African-American leader to defend these young men. You want the audience to see that racism is alive and well in this country and that it is important to create an oversight committee to monitor and avoid these situations in the future.

Opinion Journalist: You are a local conservative talk show host. You believe that this civil rights leader, who has a long history of race baiting, is using this as another opportunity to boost his stature in the community. You think that this was just another fight among boys and that racism had little to do with it. You think that the civil rights leader is blowing this issue out of proportion. You want to pressure him into admitting that he is receiving some type of personal gain.

Spinning The Facts

Take a set of facts. Create 3 different headlines from three completely different perspectives (liberal, conservative and unbiased reporter.) When writing from the liberals and conservative perspectives, do your best to demonize the opposing point pf view while making your side look favorable. When writing as the unbiased reporter, do your best to present what happened using the most sensational headline without distorting the facts.

Example:

Facts: A new abortion clinic is set to open in a predominately black neighborhood in the inner city. A pro-life group, consisting of all-white members based in the suburbs, has announced that it will protest the grand opening. A pro-choice group, consisting of primarily white members, has announced that it will hold a rally in support of the grand opening. The agency admits that it receives taxpayer funding, but none of the funding is used specifically for abortions. What should the headlines be?

Liberal: Suburban Conservatives Plan To Prevent Minority Women From Receiving Vital Health Services"
Conservative: "Liberal Groups Use Taxpayer Funds To Abort Minority Children"
Unbiased Reporter: "The New Inner-City Abortion Clinic Opens With Controversy"
As a reader, how does each headline make you feel? What emotions do each headline conjure?

Situation #1

Facts: The graduation rate for black males in your community is presently 25%. After two decades of declining graduation rates for black males, the local school board has announced that it will use offer educational vouchers for black males only. The district spends roughly $10,000 annually per pupil. The maximum award that a student can receive is $5,000. The vouchers can be used towards any private school in the county. Parents are responsible to pay for any costs that exceed the $5,000 voucher. The student must be accepted into the private school. The district teachers union opposes the program. The district announced a maximum of 10% of the county budget can be used towards the program.

Liberal:

Conservative:

Unbiased Reporter:

As a reader, how does each headline make you feel? What emotions do each headline conjure?

Situation #2

Facts: Three teenagers attempt to rob a convenience store late one night by pulling guns on a store owner. The store owner cooperates with the robbers by giving them all of the money from the register. The teenagers then walk away. The store owner then calls their attention before they leave the store. When they turn around and face him, he shoots several rounds from his pistol killing two of them and severely injuring the other. One of the suspects has a history of violent crime while the other two had absolutely no criminal record.

Liberal:

Conservative:

Unbiased Reporter:

As a reader, how does each headline make you feel? What emotions do each headline conjure?

Situation #3

Facts: A local manufacturer of consumer goods is having a labor dispute. The company has been struggling to remain profitable due to the economic slowdown. In order to prevent layoffs, the company has frozen raises and have not replaced any retired workers. Both sides made concessions during the last collective bargaining agreement. The workers have also struggled in the economy and have demanded raises. The union leadership made a statement that their members have suffered during the recession and cannot afford to concede any more. The owner of the company released a statement saying that he has conceded enough and is willing to retire and shutdown the company instead of making any more concessions to the union leadership.

Liberal:

Conservative:

Unbiased Reporter:

As a reader, how does each headline make you feel? What emotions do each headline conjure?

Situation #4

Fact: One of the local inner-city neighborhoods is now a thriving residential area. The crime rate has significantly dropped over the last year and people are beginning to spend more time outside. For the last 20 years, this neighborhood was known as the worst area in the city because of high murder rates, violent crime, vandalism, drug dealing and prostitution. The mayor campaigned to take a tough stance on crime. Since her election the police have increased patrols, walked neighborhoods, constantly approach suspicious individuals and engage known gang members and people with criminal history. The local civil liberties organization is suing the city stating that the police are harassing citizens and racially profiling. None of the members of the civil liberties organization live in the neighborhood. However, people in the neighborhood, especially senior citizens, have applauded the work of the mayor and have no problems with the police tactics.

Liberal:

Conservative:

Unbiased Reporter:

As a reader, how does each headline make you feel? What emotions do each headline conjure?

Situation #5

Fact: A prominent local minister and community activist that promotes family values finds his personal life in the news. He has traveled the country preaching abstinence and the value of marriage. After a dispute with his best friend and confidante, it was revealed that he enjoys watching Internet pornography. After intense scrutiny, he reveals that he is indeed addicted to Internet pornography in the privacy of his home. However, the only pornography he watches is heterosexual adults. He has no history of criminal sexual deviance or adultery of any kind. Local leaders have called for his resignation as pastor of the church, and his resignation on several community-based boards and commissions.

Liberal:

Conservative:

Unbiased Reporter:

As a reader, how does each headline make you feel? What emotions do each headline conjure?

Situation #6

Fact: A prominent manufacturer and one of the city's biggest employers just purchased a large amount of land that it plans to use as a dump. They have admitted that they will deposit chemical waste there. They have secured all of the government permits needed and have produced studies from noted scientists that their plans will not have any negative affect on neighboring communities or the local ecosystem. One of the communities close by the site is considered "low-income." Many of the residents work for the company. Leaders in the community have supported the company's decision. However, environmental groups vehemently oppose the company's site plans. They believe that dumping waste there could affect the health of residents and have long-term adverse health and environmental effects. They have organized boycotts and political opposition.

Liberal:

Conservative:

Unbiased Reporter:

As a reader, how does each headline make you feel? What emotions do each headline conjure?

Index

1 "Amazon.com: 40 More Years: How the Democrats Will Rule the Next Generation (9781416569893): James Carville, Rebecca Buckwalter-Poza: Books." Amazon.com: Online Shopping for Electronics, Apparel, Computers, Books, DVDs & More. Web. 09 Jan. 2011. <http://www.amazon.com/40-More-Years-Democrats-Generation/dp/1416569898>.

2 "The Fix - Election 2010: Republicans Net 60 House Seats, 6 Senate Seats and 7 Governorships." Blog Directory (washingtonpost.com). Web. 09 Jan. 2011. <http://voices.washingtonpost.com/thefix/morning-fix/2010-election-republican-score.html>.

3 Jacobs, Jeremy P. "Devastation: GOP Picks Up 680 State Leg. Seats - Hotline On Call." Hotline On Call. Web. 08 Jan. 2011. <http://hotlineoncall.nationaljournal.com/archives/2010/11/devastation-gop.php>.

4 Bergo, Sandy. "A Wealth of Advice" The Center for Public Integrity September 26, 2006 http://projects.publicintegrity.org/consultants/report.aspx?aid=533

5 "The Federalist #51." Constitution Society Home Page. Web. 09 Jan. 2011. <http://www.constitution.org/fed/federa51.htm>.

6 "Propaganda." Study Unit. History Study Center. ProQuest LLC. 1 Dec. 2010 <http://www.historystudycenter.com/>.

7 Populism: http://en.wikipedia.org/wiki/Populism

8 Bowman, John. "The History of The American Presidency." North Dayton, MA: World Publications Group, Inc. 1998.

9 "Communism." 2010. The History Channel website. Oct 22 2010, 12:32 http://www.history.com/topics/communism.

[10] Olsen, James Stewart. Encyclopedia of the Industrial Revolution. Greenwood Publishing Group, 2002. pp. 153-154

[11] "Communism." 2010. *The History Channel website.* Oct 22 2010, 12:32 http://www.history.com/topics/communism.

[12] Ibid.

[13] VANACORE, ANDREW. "US newspaper circulation down 8.7 percent." Associated Press. April 26, 2010 http://www.breitbart.com/article.php?id=D9FARMS01&show_article=1

[14] Ibid
[15] Ibid.

[16] Republican Revolution: http://en.wikipedia.org/wiki/Republican_Revolution

[17] "Senator Jay Rockefeller Wishes FCC Would Shut Down Fox News." FoxNews.com November 18, 2010 http://www.foxnews.com/politics/2010/11/18/sen-rockefeller-wishes-fcc-shut-fox-news/?test=latestnews

[18] Ibid
[19] Raju, Manu. "Reid creates special job for Schumer" Politico November 15, 2010 http://www.politico.com/news/stories/1110/45148.html

[20] Ibid.
[21] "Remarks by the President at Hampton University Commencement." The White House. Web. 09 Jan. 2011. <http://www.whitehouse.gov/the-press-office/remarks-president-hampton-university-commencement>.

[22] Stein, Sam. "Obama: I Would Not Have Nominated Clarence Thomas." Breaking News and Opinion on The Huffington Post. 16 Aug. 2008. Web. 18 Feb. 2011. <http://www.huffingtonpost.com/2008/08/16/obama-i-would-not-have-no_n_119366.html>.

[23] Levi, Michelle. "White House Says Obama Will Not Allow D.C. School Vouchers To Expire" CBSnews.com March 11, 2009 http://www.cbsnews.com/8301-503544_162-4860043-503544.html

[24] Pope, Justin. "Obama's Education Budget Cuts $85 Mil from HBCUs." BlackAmericaWeb.com May 11, 2009 http://www.blackamericaweb.com/?q=articles/news/the_state_of_black_america_news/92 29/1

[25] Levi, Edward H. An Introduction to Legal Reasoning. Chicago: University of Chicago, 1949.

[26] "Ohio Homeless Driven to Polls to Vote Obama - Politics | Republican Party | Democratic Party | Political Spectrum - FOXNews.com." FoxNews.com - Breaking News | Latest News | Current News. Web. 08 Jan. 2011. <http://www.foxnews.com/story/0,2933,433681,00.html>.

[27] Mccormack, John. "Alaska CBS Affiliate: We Have to Find a Child Molester at Joe Miller's Rally | The Weekly Standard." The Weekly Standard | A Weekly Conservative Magazine and Blog of News and Opinion. Web. 08 Jan. 2011.

<http://www.weeklystandard.com/blogs/alaska-cbs-affiliate-we-have-find-child-molester-joe-millers-rally_513401.html>.

[28] Ibid.

[29] Watkins, Dr. Boyce. "BlackNews.com - Black Mother Sentenced To Prison For Sending Kids To White School District." *BlackNews.com - Black News | African American News | Black History.* 26 Jan. 2011. Web. 28 Jan. 2011.
<http://www.blacknews.com/news/black_mother_jailed_sending_kids_white_school101.sh tml>.

[30] Levi, Michelle. "White House Says Obama Will Not Allow D.C. School Vouchers To Expire - Political Hotsheet - CBS News." *Breaking News Headlines: Business, Entertainment & World News - CBS News.* 9 Mar. 2009. Web. 28 Jan. 2011. <http://www.cbsnews.com/8301-503544_162-4860043-503544.html>.

[31] Scott, Carol. "3 Ways You Can Help Kelley Williams-Bolar, Mom Jailed For Protecting Her Kids." *Education | Change.org.* 27 Jan. 2011. Web. 28 Jan. 2011.
<http://education.change.org/blog/view/3_ways_you_can_help_kelley_williams-bolar_mom_jailed_for_protecting_her_kids>.

[32] "Jobs and Economic Justice | Representative Nancy Pelosi | Representing the 8th District of California." Representative Nancy Pelosi | Representing the 8th District of California. Web. 08 Jan. 2011. <http://pelosi.house.gov/special-issues/jobs-and-economic-justice.shtml>.

[33] "Family Values - Key Issues." United States Senator Jim DeMint. Web. 08 Jan. 2011. <http://demint.senate.gov/public/index.cfm?p=FamilyValues>.

[34] "Echo Chamber (media)." Wikipedia, the Free Encyclopedia. Web. 08 Jan. 2011. <http://en.wikipedia.org/wiki/Echo_chamber_(media)>.

[35] "Lenin Quotes - The Quotations Page." The Quotations Page - Your Source for Famous Quotes. Web. 08 Jan. 2011. <http://www.quotationspage.com/quotes/Lenin/>.

[36] "Media Montage: Obama Brought the Economy Back from the Brink." RushLimbaugh.com Home. Web. 08 Jan. 2011.
<http://www.rushlimbaugh.com/home/daily/site_071910/content/01125107.guest.html>.

[37] Smith, Sydney. "235 Journalists, News Organization Employees Made Political Contributions, 65% $ to Democrats" StinkyJournalism.org September 21, 2010 http://www.stinkyjournalism.org/editordetail.php?id=875

[38] Ibid.

[39] Malcolm, Andrew. "Do journalists' political donations (mostly Democratic) = news bias?" The Los Angeles Times July 26, 2008
http://latimesblogs.latimes.com/washington/2008/07/media-politics.html

[40] Ibid.
[41] Pew Research Center "Canvassing Campaign Media: An Analysis of Time, Tone and Topics" October 22, 2008
http://pewresearch.org/pubs/1001/campaign-media

[42] Smith, Sydney. "235 Journalists, News Organization Employees Made Political Contributions, 65% $ to Democrats" StinkyJournalism.org September 21, 2010 http://www.stinkyjournalism.org/editordetail.php?id=875

[43] "Dr. Carter G. Woodson." AALBC.com The #1 Site for African American Literature - Author Profiles, Book Reviews, Interviews and More. Web. 09 Jan. 2011. <http://aalbc.com/authors/carterg.htm>.

[44] Curry, Tom. "Biden defends Obama's tax deal with GOP" msnbc.com December 19, 2010 http://www.msnbc.msn.com/id/40733482/ns/politics/

[45] "FAQ » Cpusa." Home » Cpusa. Web. 21 Feb. 2011. <http://cpusa.org/faq/>.

[46] "Why the Wealth Gap Between Blacks and Whites Is Growing." Home | The Root. Web. 09 Jan. 2011. <http://www.theroot.com/views/black-white-wealth-gap-growing>.

[47] Scruggs, Darrick H. "Being Black In America." EzineArticles Submission - Submit Your Best Quality Original Articles For Massive Exposure, Ezine Publishers Get 25 Free Article Reprints. Web. 09 Jan. 2011. <http://ezinearticles.com/?Being-Black-In-America&id=872120>.

[48] Hallman, Charles. "By 2011 Black Buying Power to Hit Trillion-Dollar Mark" Minnesota Spokesman-Recorder January 10, 2008 http://news.newamericamedia.org/news/view_article.html?article_id=990c03344a0ec68e9e dcfcaaa70e7563

[49] McAuliff, Michael. "Now George Soros Backs Media Matters; Beck Calls It a 'Bounty'" New York Daily News October 20, 2010 http://www.nydailynews.com/blogs/dc/2010/10/now-george-soros-backs-media-m.html#ixzz14upqGqB6

[50] Hoft , Jim. " Protesters at 'Anti-Hate' Rally Call Breitbart Homosexual, Spit on Him" Breitbart TV http://www.breitbart.tv/protesters-at-anti-hate-rally-call-breitbart-homosexual-spit-on-him/

[51] NUNNALLY, DERRICK "5 charged in GOP tire slashings" Milwaukee Journal Sentinel January 25, 2005 http://www3.jsonline.com/story/index.aspx?id=295825

[52] Berger, Judson. "Activist Group Puts Bounty on Chamber of Commerce CEO" FOXNews.com December 07, 2009 |http://www.foxnews.com/politics/2009/12/07/liberal-group-offers-reward-information-chamber-boss/

[53] "Blog Wants Celebs to Help Oust Lieberman's Wife From Susan Komen Ambassadorship" FOXNews.com December 14, 2009 http://www.foxnews.com/politics/2009/12/14/blog-wants-celebs-help-oust-liebermans-wife-breast-cancer-cure-group/

[54] "Obama: 'We Bring a Gun'" THE NEW YORK TIMES June 14, 2008 http://thecaucus.blogs.nytimes.com/2008/06/14/obama-we-bring-a-gun/

[55] Associated Press. "Protest Cancels Coulter Speech in Ottawa" FoxNews.com March 24, 2010 http://www.foxnews.com/politics/2010/03/24/protest-cancels-coulter-speech-ottawa/

[56] "Rock the Vote Asks Supporters to Withhold Sex to Pass Health Care Reform" FoxNews.com
December 21, 2009
http://www.foxnews.com/politics/2009/12/21/rock-vote-asks-supporters-withhold-sex-pass-health-care-reform/?utm_source=feedburner&utm_medium=feed&utm_campaign=Feed%253A+foxnews%252Fpolitics+%2528FOXNews.com+-+Politics%2529

[57] Cook, Dave. "Howard Dean: Tea Party Is 'last Gasp' of Generation That Fears Diversity - CSMonitor.com." *The Christian Science Monitor - CSMonitor.com.* 5 Jan. 2001. Web. 09 Jan. 2011. <http://www.csmonitor.com/USA/Politics/monitor_breakfast/2011/0105/Howard-Dean-tea-party-is-last-gasp-of-generation-that-fears-diversity>.

[58] Gordon, Meryl. "The Unlikely Rise of Howard Dean." New York Magazine -- NYC Guide to Restaurants, Fashion, Nightlife, Shopping, Politics, Movies. 24 Feb. 2003. Web. 08 Mar. 2011. <http://nymag.com/nymetro/news/politics/national/n_8376/>.

[59] "Conservative vs. Liberal Beliefs" StudentNewsDaily.com
Copyright 2005 (revised 2010)
http://www.studentnewsdaily.com/other/conservative-vs-liberal-beliefs/

[60] Ibid.

[61] "Racism." The American Heritage® New Dictionary of Cultural Literacy, Third Edition. Houghton Mifflin Company, 2005. 07 Jan. 2011. <Dictionary.com
http://dictionary.reference.com/browse/racism>.

[62] Breen, Bill. "Who Do You Love?" Fast Company December 19, 2007
http://www.fastcompany.com/magazine/115/features-who-do-you-love.html

[63] Ibid.

[64] Ibid.

[65] Ibid.

[66] Ibid.

[67] Jeffrey, Terence P. "Conservatives Now Outnumber Liberals in All 50 States, Says Gallup Poll" CNSNews.com August 17, 2009
http://www.cnsnews.com/news/article/52602

[68] Klepper, Michael. "Getting Your Message Out: How to Use, and Survive Radio and Television Air Time" Prentice Hall, 1984.

[69] Krotz, Joanna L. "6 Tips for Taking Control in Media Interviews." Microsoft Corporation. Web. 09 Jan. 2011. <http://www.microsoft.com/business/en-us/resources/ArticleReader/website/default.aspx?Print=1&ArticleId=tipsfortakingcontrolinmediainterviews>.

[70] Berger, Jason. "Berger: Teaching Media Interview Skills ." Lamar.ColoState.EDU. May 1992. Web. 09 Jan. 2011. <http://lamar.colostate.edu/~aejmcpr/27berger.htm>.

[71] Mooney, Alexander. "'I'm Through,' Palin Says – CNN Political Ticker - CNN.com Blogs." CNN Political Ticker - CNN.com Blogs. 25 Mar. 2011. Web. <http://politicalticker.blogs.cnn.com/2011/03/24/im-through-palin-says/>.

[72] CNN LARRY KING WEEKEND "Encore Presentation: Interview With Ronald Reagan" Aired July 5, 2003

http://quiz.cnn.com/TRANSCRIPTS/0307/05/lklw.00.html

73 PoliticsNewsPolitics. "Greta w/ Sheila Jackson-Lee: "You're Not Listening - Again!" 13 August 2009 YouTube. Accessed on 5 January 2011.

74 Rescuetruth. "Alvin Greene Answers Nearly Every Question With "DeMint Started the Recession" YouTube. Accessed on 5 January 2011.

75 Berger, Jason. "Berger: Teaching Media Interview Skills ." Lamar.ColoState.EDU. May 1992. Web. 09 Jan. 2011. <http://lamar.colostate.edu/~aejmcpr/27berger.htm>.

76 "Expert Interview Body Language Tips." Job Interviews. Free Interview Questions and Answers and Job Interview Tips. Web. 09 Jan. 2011. <http://www.best-job-interview.com/interview-body-language.html>.

77 Krotz, Joanna L. "6 Tips for Taking Control in Media Interviews." Microsoft Corporation. Web. 09 Jan. 2011. <http://www.microsoft.com/business/en-us/resources/ArticleReader/website/default.aspx?Print=1&ArticleId=tipsfortakingcontrolinmediainterviews>.

78 Keeney, Daniel. "Fundamentals of Media Interview Skills: Facial Expression." Famous Entrepreneurs, Small Business, Young, Successful, Women, Toronto Resources. Web. 09 Jan. 2011. <http://www.evancarmichael.com/Public-Relations/213/Fundamentals-of-media-interview-skills-facial-expression.html>.

79 Saad, Lydia. "In 2010, Conservatives Still Outnumber Moderates, Liberals." Gallup.Com - Daily News, Polls, Public Opinion on Government, Politics, Economics, Management. 25 June 2010. Web. 21 Feb. 2011. <http://www.gallup.com/poll/141032/2010-conservatives-outnumber-moderates-liberals.aspx>.

80 Field, Andy. "Never Repeat A Negative- When Dealing With The Media." Media Training Media Coaching Media Preparation. 2008. Web. 09 Jan. 2011. <http://www.media-training.info/Media-Training-Articles/Never-Repeat-A-Negative.html>.

81 Ibid.

82 Ibid
83 Ibid.

84 McMorris-Santoro, Evan. "New Poll Shows Rand Paul Up 13 -- And Voters Don't Like Conway's Aqua Buddha Ad" Talking Points Memo October 26, 2010, 10:00 http://tpmdc.talkingpointsmemo.com/2010/10/new-poll-shows-rand-paul-up-13.php

85 Madison, Lucy. "Christine O'Donnell Says She Regrets Witch Ad, Won't Be a Witch for Halloween" CBS news October 21, 2010
 http://www.cbsnews.com/8301-503544_162-20020279-503544.html

86 mediamatters4america. "Norah O'Donnell Stumps Palin Supporter By Asking About Palin's Support Of Bailouts" 18 November 2009. Online video clip. YouTube. Accessed on 3 January 2011.

87 Ibid.

88 "Senate GOP again kills extension of unemployment benefits" The Los Angeles Times July 1, 2010

http://articles.latimes.com/2010/jul/01/nation/la-na-0701-senate-jobless-20100701

[89] PEAR, ROBERT and HERSZENHORN, DAVID M. "Obama Hails Vote on Health Care as Answering 'the Call of History'" The New York Times March 21, 2010
http://www.nytimes.com/2010/03/22/health/policy/22health.html

[90] Ferraro, Thomas. "Republicans target Democrats on healthcare reform" Reuters March 23, 2010
http://www.reuters.com/article/idUSTRE62L5QS20100323

[91] Riley, Charles. "Obama calls for federal wage freeze" CNN Money November 29, 2010
http://money.cnn.com/2010/11/29/news/economy/federal_pay_freeze/index.htm

[92] "Democrats chip away at GOP on financial reform" Reuters Apr 16, 2010
http://www.reuters.com/article/idUSTRE63F3YY20100416

[93] Montopoli, Brian. "Republicans (and One Democrat) Block Debate on Financial Reform Bill" CBS News April 26, 2010
http://www.cbsnews.com/8301-503544_162-20003456-503544.html

[94] Mcauliff, Michael and Bazinet, Kenneth R. "President Obama slams obstructionist Republicans at GOP issues retreat" New York Daily News January 30th 2010
http://www.nydailynews.com/news/politics/2010/01/30/2010-01-30_baltimore_chop_for_gop_president_slams_obstructionist_republicans_on_their_home_.html#ixzz1AHbnPRAW

[95] Mcauliff, Michael. "Obama tells GOP it's bad time for 'no' as meetings with Republicans loom" New York Daily News November 15, 2010
http://www.nydailynews.com/news/politics/2010/11/15/2010-11-15_obama_tells_gop_its_bad_time_for_no.html

[96] Altman, Alex. "The GOP House's Opening Act: Making a Statement — or Making a Mockery?" Time Magazine January 5, 2011
http://www.time.com/time/politics/article/0,8599,2040805,00.html#ixzz1AHcxSXhO

[97] Horowitz, Jason. "Recitation of Constitution set in House renews debate over Founders' intentions" The Washington Post January 4, 2011
http://www.washingtonpost.com/wpdyn/content/article/2011/01/04/AR2011010404652.html

[98] SEIB, GERALD F. "Democrats Try to Crack Mystery of the Missing Voters" The Wall Street Journal November 23, 2010
http://online.wsj.com/article/SB10001424052748703559504575630453372436666.html

[99] "PROMISES, PROMISES: GOP drops some out of the gate" Associated Press January 6, 2011
http://www.google.com/hostednews/ap/article/ALeqM5j9c-FTokgMpPeCrAWl-nb5Y89g8A?docId=1d2f7dee49e1440786b6f55442a8a802

[100] FOUHY, BETH. "Anonymous donors spent $132M on 2010 campaign ads" MSNBC December 10, 2010
http://www.msnbc.msn.com/id/40608858/ns/politics-decision_2010/

[101] PACE, JULIE. "Obama Exhorts Republicans to Put Politics Aside" ABC News January 4, 2011
http://abcnews.go.com/US/wireStory?id=12539160

[102] "David Letterman Made Fun of Philanderers For Years as he Pursued Own Affairs"
Fox News October 07, 2009
http://www.foxnews.com/entertainment/2009/10/07/david-letterman-fun-philanderers-years-pursued-affairs/

[103] DEAN, CHARLES J. "In Black Belt: McCain wins hearts not votes"
The Birmingham News April 22, 2008

[104] "Pelosi: Incoming Speaker Boehner 'Known to Cry'" Fox News November 20, 2010
http://www.foxnews.com/politics/2010/11/20/pelosi-incoming-speaker-boehner-known/

[105] PRESTON, JULIA. "Immigration Vote Leaves Obama's Policy in Disarray" The New York
Times December 18, 2010
http://www.nytimes.com/2010/12/19/us/politics/19dream.html

[106] Stone, Peter and Isikoff, Michael. "How Wall St. execs bankrolled GOP victory"
MSNBC January 5, 2011
http://www.msnbc.msn.com/id/40913123/ns/politics/

[107] Ignatius, David. "Is Darrell Issa the new Joe McCarthy?" The Washington Post
January 5, 2011
http://voices.washingtonpost.com/postpartisan/2011/01/is_darrell_issa_the_new_joe_mc.html

[108] Washington, Jesse. "Minorities ride GOP wave to groundbreaking wins" Associated Press
November 3, 2011
http://news.yahoo.com/s/ap/20101103/ap_on_el_ge/us_election_minorities

www.ingramcontent.com/pod-product-compliance
Lightning Source LLC
Chambersburg PA
CBHW020242290526
45784CB00003B/1081